### *Everything you need to know about volunteer work in Latin America*

Argentina, Belize, Bolivia, Brazil, Chile,
Costa Rica, Ecuador, El Salvador,
Guatemala, Honduras, Mexico,
Nicaragua, Panama,
Peru, Venezuela,
Uruguay

# ANNE-MARIE DINGEMANS PEREZ MBA

Volunteer Work Latin America
Everything you need to know about volunteer work in Latin America

First Edition
Copyright© 2012 by Anne-Marie Dingemans Perez MBA

All rights reserved.
No part of this book may be reproduced, scanned,
or distributed in any printed or electronic
form without permission. Please do not
participate in or encourage piracy
of copyrighted material
in violation of the
author's rights.
Purchase only authorized editions.

For more information
please visit:
www.VolunteerWorkLatinAmerica.com
or contact:
info@VolunteerWorkLatinAmerica.com

While the author has made every effort to provide accurate information
and internet addresses at the time of publication, neither the publisher nor the author
assumes any responsibility for errors, or for changes that occur after publication.

Limit of Liability: While the publisher and author have used their best efforts in preparing this book, they make
no representations or warranties regarding the accuracy or completeness of the contents of this book. The advice and
information given in this book may not be suitable for your situation. Neither the publisher nor author shall be liable for
any damages or mishaps incurred while engaging in volunteer work in Latin America.

ISBN-13: 978-1475053852
ISBN-10: 1475053851

Printed in the United States of America

COVER AND INTERIOR DESIGN BY SEBASTIÁN PÉREZ

For Sebastian
Mentor. Coach. Facilitator.
You are the secret ingredient in everything I do.

# Table of contents

# 1 Why working as a volunteer?  1

1.1 What is volunteer work?   2

1.2 What can volunteers do?   3
    1.2.1 Community Service   4
    1.2.2 Nature Conservancy   4
    1.2.3 Professional   5

1.3 Reasons for volunteering   6

1.4 Advantages and Disadvantages of Volunteering in Latin America   7
    1.4.1 Advantages:   7
    1.4.2 Disadvantages:   8

1.5 Volunteering vs. Interning   10

1.6 Which organizations accept volunteers and why? Understanding the 'business' of volunteering: why do organizations accept volunteers?   11

1.7 Your skills   17
    1.7.1 Professional skills   17
    1.7.2 Soft skills   18
    1.7.3 Language skills   19

1.8 Can I expect compensation?   20

1.9 Long-term vs. short-term volunteering   24

1.10 Matching the volunteer work with your needs   25

1.11 Latin American Volunteer destination guide   31

Table of contents                                                                 iii

# 2 Finding a Volunteer position · 49

## 2.1 Through Agencies/ Intermediaries · 50
2.1.1 What is an agency or intermediary? · 51
2.1.2 How do agencies/ intermediaries work · 51
2.1.3 What can you expect from an agency/ intermediary · 53
2.1.4 Advantages/ Disadvantages · 55
2.1.5 Costs/ Cost structure · 56
2.1.6 Evaluating agencies/intermediaries · 59
2.1.7 How to find an agency or intermediary · 60
2.1.8 List of Agencies · 61
2.1.9 Tips on applying · 65

## 2.2 Intermediaries in the host country · 67
2.2.1 What is an in-country intermediary? · 67
2.2.2 How do in-country intermediaries work? · 67
2.2.3 What can you expect from an in-country agency/ intermediary? · 68
2.2.4 Advantages/ Disadvantages · 70
2.2.5 Costs/ Cost structure · 71
2.2.6 Evaluating in-country agencies/intermediaries · 72
2.2.7 How to find an in-country agency/ intermediary · 73
2.2.8 List of in-country Agencies/ Intermediaries · 73
2.2.9 Tips on applying · 77

## 2.3 Going direct · 79
2.3.1 NGO's and large international organizations · 80
    2.3.1.1 What can you expect when going directly to an organization · 80
    2.3.1.2 Advantages/ Disadvantages · 80
    2.3.1.3 Costs/ Cost structure · 81
    2.3.1.4 Evaluating organizations · 82
2.3.2 Local/Grassroots organizations · 82
    2.3.2.1 What can you expect when going directly to an organization · 82
    2.3.2.2 Advantages/ Disadvantages · 84
    2.3.2.3 Costs/ Cost structure · 85
    2.3.2.4 Evaluating receiving organizations · 86
2.3.3 'Regular' (non-aid) organizations and businesses · 88
    2.3.3.1 What can you expect when going directly to an organization · 89
    2.3.3.2 Advantages/ Disadvantages · 90
    2.3.3.3 Costs/ Cost structure · 90
    2.3.3.4 Evaluating 'regular' organizations and businesses · 90
2.3.4 How to find an organization · 91
2.3.5 List of organizations · 91
2.3.6 Tips on applying · 100

# 3 Preparing For Working In Latin America 103

## 3.1 Culture — 104
### 3.1.1 Now, what is culture shock, then? — 104
### 3.1.2 What is culture? — 107
### 3.1.3 High vs. Low context communication — 112

## 3.2 Language — 114
### 3.2.1 At home or in-country? — 114
### 3.2.2 Some tips on language learning: — 116
### 3.2.3 Just in case — 118

## 3.3 Finances — 119
### 3.3.1 Currency — 119
### 3.3.2 How to get to your money — 120
### 3.3.3 Paying and Negotiating — 121
### 3.3.4 Tourist vs. Local prices — 123
### 3.3.5 Earning money in Latin America — 123

## 3.4 Logistics — 124
### 3.4.1 Do you need a visa? — 124
### 3.4.2 Passport — 126
### 3.4.3 Flight — 126
### 3.4.4 Accommodation — 128
#### 3.4.4.1 Host families — 128
#### 3.4.4.2 Residences — 129
#### 3.4.4.3 Shared apartments — 129
#### 3.4.4.4 Hotel or private apartments — 130
### 3.4.5 Insurance — 130

## 3.5 Health — 131
### 3.5.1 Vaccinations — 131
### 3.5.2 Malaria, Dengue fever and other diseases — 132
### 3.5.3 (Prescription) Medications — 133
### 3.5.4 Food & Drink — 134
### 3.5.5 If you get ill — 136

## 3.6 Safety — 138
### 3.6.1 Petty theft — 138
### 3.6.2 Getting robbed — 140
### 3.6.3 Women travelers — 141
### 3.6.4 Specific challenges for volunteers — 142

## Online Bonus Material

Unavoidable but necessary -
you'll have to spend many hours
chasing documents, calling people
and filling out forms
before you can leave for your trip.

This ebook will help you go through the preparations
with less stress, knowing exactly which are the
101 things you need to do before you leave

Register at
www.VolunteerWorkLatinAmerica.com
and get the free ebook:
101 THINGS YOU NEED TO DO BEFORE YOU LEAVE

# 1
## Why working as a volunteer?

## 1.1 What is volunteer work?

> The definition of volunteer work is that you donate your time, knowledge and skills to a particular cause, without receiving any monetary compensation for your time and services.

When we speak of international volunteer work, we talk about people leaving their own homes, jobs and life behind and move to another country to contribute to a cause in that country. Their stay is almost always temporary and can often even be classified as short stays.

Volunteer work is not a vacation in the sense that the volunteers make a commitment to the project which requires them to work at that project during specific hours. For most, the commitment level is equal to or superior to that of a 'regular' job. So even if you are volunteering part-time you don't have much flexibility to take time off to travel, sleeping in, or just having an off-day.

Volunteer work is also not comparable to regular jobs as the particular position of the volunteer sets him aside from regular employees, for example in the sense that the standard extrinsic motivation mechanism of 'if you don't do as I say I will fire you and you won't receive your salary' doesn't apply. The idea is that you want to do this and that your intrinsic motivation ensures your responsible behavior.

Also, as international volunteer positions are generally short to very short term, there is less time for a volunteer to be trained in his duties, to get to know the whole organization and to become fully integrated in the team.

## 1.2 What can volunteers do?

As you will have understood from the definition of volunteer work in the above paragraph, whether your job is qualified as 'volunteer work' doesn't depend on the tasks you perform but on the fact wether you're getting paid or not!

This means that if you want to volunteer, in theory all jobs, positions and responsibilities are open to you. In this book we discuss international volunteering in Latin America, and for the purpose of this book we will call volunteer work:

> Volunteer work: any position at any organization, where people can work full-time or part-time, for a relatively short period of time, and receive no or little compensation.

Cynics will say that this definition of 'little or no compensation' includes pretty much any existing job in Latin America, but we think you know what we mean. For more details on which compensation you can expect, see paragraph 1.8.

To make your search for your perfect volunteer opportunity easier, we have grouped all possible volunteer positions in three main categories: Community Service, Nature Conservancy and Professional volunteer positions.

## 1.2.1 Community Service

Under 'community service' you'll find all types of volunteer work at organizations that aim to improve the lives of the people in their community in any way.

You can think of projects that provide care for disadvantaged groups such as children, elderly, handicapped, addicted or homeless people. This care can range from a soup kitchen, via day care and organized activities to centers where therapy and/or long-term care are given.

This category also includes programs aimed at improving the educational level of the community, through free kindergarten centers, after-school care and homework assistance, skills improvement programs for adults, etc..

Organizations aiming to improve the health of (often underprivileged) communities are also included in this section. Medical organizations such as hospitals and clinics will often accept volunteers; mostly they require relevant education and experience, but not always. Other possibilities are assisting with promotional activities, such as AIDS/HIV awareness programs, hygiene campaigns, or assistance to and information for pregnant women and nursing mothers.

## 1.2.2 Nature Conservancy

This category contains all sorts of volunteer positions related to nature, ecology and animal/wildlife preservation.

In these organizations, volunteers are often needed

to help keeping animal rescue centers and nature parks operational, which translates in lots of physical work, such as cleaning and maintenance tasks. You need to be aware that for many prospective volunteers, the idea of working with wildlife is the most seducing aspect of the volunteer experience. In reality, though, you will notice that although you should expect to have some access to the wildlife, the vast majority of your tasks will consist of supportive duties (read: cleaning!).

Most of the help needed is physical work, but you could also help the cause of conservancy organizations with office support, promotional and funding activities, or by assisting researchers.

### 1.2.3 Professional

This last category is a very broad mix of volunteer projects for which specific professional skills and/or experience is needed. Professional internships are counted in this category as well.

Think of volunteers who have just graduated from college and are taking their first step in their profession. Sometimes students who haven't yet finished their program can participate as well.

> Experienced professionals of all fields are coveted volunteers who can greatly contribute to the organization. They can help improve the knowledge base of the permanent staff, their contribution has a long-term effect.

Naturally, if your profession is in the educational, social work, health care, biology, conservancy or related fields, your desired volunteer position would also fall in the community service or nature conservancy categories. The distinguishing factor is that for professional volunteer positions education and/or professional experience is required.

## 1.3 Reasons for volunteering

Many people dream of spending some time in a foreign country and every individual has his/her unique reasons for doing so.

Before deciding to embark on a volunteer adventure, please make sure that you are aware exactly why you want to do this. If your reasons are clear for yourself, it will be much easier to find a program that suits your needs which in turn increases the probability that you'll have a wonderful experience at your chosen project.

Reasons for volunteering can be divided in two groups; first altruistic reasons, such as contributing to community development, improve the quality of life for people, knowledge transfer, environmental management and protecting the environment; and secondly personal reasons such as getting to know a different culture, personal growth, funding living abroad, learning new skills, trying out a possible new career of profession, and gaining work experience.

Most volunteers have a mix of both altruistic as more personal reasons to volunteer. This is ok! If you have purely altruistic or purely personal reasons, that is ok too. There is no right or wrong, but knowing your own reasons and goals will help you choose a project that best suits your needs.

If one of your reasons is getting to know a new culture and improve your Spanish or Portuguese language skills, then we would advice you to find a volunteer position at a locally-run organization. Big NGO's such as Habitat for Humanity or the Peace Corps do great work with the local communities, but have a Western-based organizational structure. You will learn much more about a Latin American culture if you dive in 100%, and you can achieve this by choosing an organization which is run the 'Latin way'. I warn you, and I say this from my own experience – it isn't easy to immerse yourself completely, without an escape, but it surely is effective! More on cultural differences and how to deal with culture shock in paragraph 3.1.

## 1.4 Advantages and Disadvantages of Volunteering in Latin America

### 1.4.1 Advantages:

1. There is no better way of getting to know a new culture than living it;

2. You will dramatically improve your Spanish or Portuguese language skills;

3. You will feel the satisfaction of having contributed in an altruistic way to the world;

4. Getting to know an other way of working, thinking and feeling enriches your own outlook on life;

5. You can improve your professional and personal skills;

6. You can take an insider look at a profession or industry you're contemplating working in;

7. You improve your employability by having international work experience (and having improved your language, professional and personal skills);

8. You make friends from all over the world;

9. You may come back more mature, self-assured and with a better idea what you want to do in life;

10. many, many more…..

## 1.4.2 Disadvantages:

1. You'll be committed to spending a considerable amount of time at the project. Enjoying leisure time, taking off to travel to other places, or taking part in other activities will be limited. Before committing, please think long and hard if this really is what you want to do, and commit for the shortest period you're absolutely sure of. Shortening a volunteer period can seriously inconvenience the organization, but staying longer will be welcomed!

2. If you are in intensive contact with the local population in a developing country, you are at a higher risk to contract certain diseases such as Hepatitis, Tuberculosis, Typhoid, Cholera, Parasites and bacteria. Make sure you have your vaccinations and take sufficient precautions while in-country;

3. Many volunteers acutely feel their own privileged position as they are confronted with people who didn't have the same opportunities in life. Although confronting and uncomfortable, this is of course also a valuable process of personal growth;

4. You'll often be asked to work long and hard hours, performing menial tasks. This can be weary, and may make you feel like your skills are not used to the fullest. Think about what is holding you back. Maybe your language skills are not sufficient to do the work you'd most like to do? Or maybe you've committed to staying for just a few weeks so the staff may feel it is not worth the time to train you? Speak to the director or volunteer coordinator about your feelings. Also, sometimes you need to accept that your presence, taking over time-consuming tasks, frees up the time of the permanent staff members to do those tasks they normally don't have time to do. For example, if you work at a day care centre and you take care of the cleaning and washing, the permanent staff has time to give attention to the children. They are there permanently so it may be more beneficial for the children to form a bond with them than with the volunteer who leaves after a while;

5. You may feel that your contribution has no lasting effect on the community. It can help to realize that while you are there, you are having a great impact, and when you leave, another volunteer can come and take your place. All of the volunteers together have a strong and lasting effect on the community. Also, you

can continue to be involved with the project once you're back in your country, for example by collecting donations, generating publicity and media exposure for your project, or acting as an ambassador or finding and preparing future volunteers.

## 1.5 Volunteering vs. Interning

Often, the terms 'volunteering' and 'interning' are used interchangeably. If a difference is made, it will be that an internship position is meant for people in the later stages or having just finished a college or university degree who want to gain work experience in their professional field. The focus will be more on the intern acquiring and improving his/her professional skills, than on the volunteer offering a helping hand and/or transferring knowledge to the receiving organization.

Volunteers with (or studying for) a law, business, economics or similar degree will be more likely to see postings for 'internships' than those who have studied degrees in technical, social sciences or health care fields. We advise you not to limit yourself to a term and look at the actual job description before deciding to apply for a position.

When you are looking for an international internship and you must have certain paperwork in order for your school to approve your credits, proceed with care! Investigate very carefully what you need to submit, who needs to sign documents, in which language they need to be and when you have to have your paperwork in order. Latin American culture is based on personal relationships and personal contacts and it may be very difficult to entice your contact person to invest time and effort in preparing paperwork before he/she has ever met you in person. Once on-site it will be much easier to obtain what you need, but generally you should expect a lower level of detail and a less strict adherence to protocol and procedures than what we are used to in the Anglo-Saxon and Germanic cultures. They also tend to be less concerned with deadlines.

The amount of experience your school has with students interning in Latin America, and the experience of your employer with receiving interns from other countries will greatly influence how these issues are dealt with. This is actually one of the situations where I strongly recommend working with an agency, preferably an agency from your own country, as they have established relationships with employers and can therefore place you in a project that meet your and your school's needs, and act on your behalf if you need to get something done before you travel!

## 1.6 Which organizations accept volunteers and why? Understanding the 'business' of volunteering: why do organizations accept volunteers?

You probably know enough of Latin America to be aware that most countries have a low GDP, that there is a sharp division between rich and poor and that the economic prognoses are not very optimistic. You can imagine what this means for the average business in these countries and especially for community service organizations. Government funding is scarce, insecure and subject to corruption. Many organizations are dependent on local and international donations, and are continually struggling to get by.

Perpetual underfunding, for both non-profit as commercial organizations and businesses is a fact of life. It is wonderful to see that even, of perhaps especially in, the poorest communities there are lots of local volunteers who help these projects. At the same time, most of the work will be done by paid employees. For some of these employees it's just another job, others are deeply committed. Sometimes the organization can afford to hire highly qualified staff, more often than not most of the work is done by un- or lower schooled staff (as they receive lower salaries).

> Now, the advantage of receiving a volunteer is obvious – how incredible is it that a stranger offers to come and help you for a few weeks or months?!?! Your help will be very much appreciated and makes a great difference. Your presence can free up the permanent staff from some of their day-to-day duties to make time for long-term improvement. Or maybe you will be the person that sets a new idea in motion while the permanent staff keeps things running. If you have training and experience in the field of operation of the organization you can really make a difference, especially in those organizations that cannot afford to hire enough qualified personnel. You can bring knowledge, fresh insights and the newest techniques to an organization.

If you just finished high school or do not have relevant professional training and experience, your help, your energy and your commitment are very important to any organization where you go to help. On the other hand, any time a new person comes to work in an organization, that person will have to be introduced, shown around and trained to perform his/her duties. This always takes a lot of time, and even more so if the person comes from another culture, doesn't speak the language very well, and/or does not have prior work experience in the job he/she needs to do. Every organization, when deciding whether to accept a volunteer will make this calculation. Is the benefit of having a person help us greater than the effort in training this person? You can imagine that if you do not speak the local language, have no experience, and want to commit for 2 weeks only, the result of this mental calculation may not be favorable for you! So, when applying to a volunteer position, think about your worth to the organization.

Sometimes the decision is not as logical as I have described above. Latin American cultures are more hierarchical than Anglo-Saxon and Germanic cultures, and a person 'higher-up' can decide that a project will not accept volunteers. In such a situation the location director cannot do much about that decision. I have experienced that an orphanage run by a catholic order, which had been receiving the help of foreign volunteers for years, has to stop this, literally from one day to the next when a new bishop was appointed who decreed that volunteers were 'not needed'. No logic, no explanation, this was just how it was going to be..... Incredible for most of us, but these things actually happen. So don't feel bad if you're rejected, or if your application is canceled for no logical reason. Sometimes there simply is no good explanation.

The same hierarchical culture can lead to the situation where the directors of a project or organization subscribe to the idea of receiving volunteers, but forget, or don't find it necessary, to communicate the reasons behind this decision to the employees. If you arrive to work at an organization, your presence can be felt as something management pushed on the employees. They will have to take the  time to explain your duties, they will work alongside you, maybe have to help you with your language learning, but they might not be aware of the benefits to the organization. The concept of volunteering is still fairly unknown in Latin America, so you can't hold it against your colleagues if they are not quite sure what to do with you.

 There have been situations where volunteers were discouraged to do anything, and told to sit in a corner and observe. When asked, it turned out that the staff had heard from the management that volunteers were foreigners who came to work but weren't getting paid. Wonderful hosts as they are, the women working at this day care centre made sure the volunteers were as comfortable as possible and didn't have to lift a finger. This is how you treat guests! Once we realized that this basic misunderstanding was the source of the volunteers feeling superfluous and useless and we let the director know, a good conversation between the in-country volunteer coordinator, the director and the staff of the project cleared up the misunderstanding and although the staff found the concept of working for no money a little odd, they decided to go for it and with practice learned to enjoy the extra help without feeling guilty!

# 1 • Why working as a volunteer?

For some organizations there is an additional reason for accepting international volunteers. When allowing volunteers to work in the organization, a person gets a real good feeling for the goals but also the struggles of the project. Often, volunteers stay committed to the organization's goals even when they are back in their own country, and will continue to support the cause through donations. Unfortunately, there are projects which have realized this 'willingness' of international volunteers to financially support organizations, and have established obligatory donations for every volunteer. Apparently there are enough people so charmed with the idea of working in an orphanage that they are willing to pay not only their own room and board, but also a fee for the privilege of working there. We strongly oppose these practices. If volunteers are accepted just for the money that they bring, what is their help, their presence doing for the organization? Will you really have a good time, learn new things, and connect with the people? Or will you be 'tolerated' while you keep paying?

Then, there is the danger of corruption. Corruption is a fact of life in Latin America and a regular occurrence. If you give money to a project please try to make sure that your money goes where it is supposed to go. We are not saying all organizations are corrupt, of course not, but corruption does exist and some people can not resist the temptation to make 'easy money', especially off foreigners.

> When volunteering, you may run into situations where people assume you are limitlessly rich. If you've been saving up for years to come to Latin America, and just barely can make ends meet, this can be a really frustrating experience. It can make you feel like people

> consider you to be a cash machine, or that you're always expected to pay for everything, or you may even doubt if friendships are completely genuine or if there is a bit of opportunism involved. These are all very legitimate thoughts and feelings, and in my opinion about the only downside of working in Latin America. Also, it's unavoidable.

To be able to deal with this reality, it's important for you to understand the point of view of the other. You know that in Latin America there is a very small middle class. In general, people are poor (at or around the poverty line) or extremely rich. There is little middle ground. So in their view, the argument is as follows: "You're not poor, thus you must be extremely rich". This is how the world works for many Latin Americans. If nobody told them otherwise, how can they know?. Poor people have little access to education, can't afford to travel, don't usually move outside of their own social circle, and see the world outside of their town through the filter of television. The only impressions they have seen from people living in the Western world are TV shows such as 'Sex and the City'. It will be nearly impossible for you to convince your conversation partner that you had to save money for your trip, that you don't live in Manhattan and that you had to work long and hard to be able to afford to come here. I still encourage you to do so. Talk about your life, show pictures of home, and explain. You will notice that if a project has been receiving volunteers for a while the staff will move toward a more faceted view.

Volunteer positions can be restricted by the laws and regulations in a country. In Peru, for example, patients cannot be seen (or rather, touched in any way) by people who are not licensed medical professionals. This law makes a lot of sense, of course, but one may doubt the logic of it when one bears in mind that many very rural areas in the country have no medical care at all, and where the help of medical or nursing students under the supervision of a Peruvian MD can make a tremendous difference. Yes, a medical student cannot even undertake non invasive tasks such as taking the blood pressure of a patient, not unless a Peruvian licensed MD is standing right next to him/her.

## 1.7 Your skills

Your skills will have a large influence on your 'marketability' for different volunteer positions. We recommend that you start making a thorough and honest list of the skills with which you can contribute to an organization. Knowing and recognizing your strengths and weaknesses will help you create a realistic picture of your options for finding an interesting position.

### 1.7.1 Professional skills

Why would an organization want your help? What do you have to offer? Even if you're not a seasoned professional yet, or haven't finished your degree, you do have professional skills. Everybody has something to offer, even if you're young and straight out of school. Can you teach English? Has your babysitting job prepared you for taking care of babies and young children? Have you been captain of the school soccer team? Are you a wizz at computers? Maybe you're a technician but would like to work in a more social environment.

Think how you can apply your strengths to a new environment. Maybe your analytical way of thinking can help the project organize their administration? Or you can do some serious maintenance on the wheelchairs. Maybe you are an accountant who would like to work with the handicapped. Then you could propose to dedicate 1 or 2 hours a day to the bookkeeping of the organization. This thinking out of the box can instantly turn you into an extremely valuable volunteer. Do you have abundant energy and don't mind working in the heat? Everybody has skills that are very useful for a prospective organization. Know them and use them!

## 1.7.2 Soft skills

As you've read in paragraph 1.6, your professional skills, your work experience, your motivation, attitude and commitment are desirable assets to the receiving organization. However, having skills is not enough; you have to be able to apply them within the organization.

How do you share knowledge, ideas, insights, feedback with the organization you are working in? You can imagine that simply stating that "the way you do things around here is completely backwards – let me show you how we do this in Europe/USA" – might not be very effective! Always remember that you are a guest, in the project, in the city, in the country. You should always show respect for the environment you are in. Even though a community may not be rich or have access to the same resources you do, that does not mean that they do not have self-respect and pride. If you step into their lives and start acting superior, you will only encounter resistance. Influencing people, teaching them, when you are in the position of unpaid, visiting guest, require extensive people skills, flexibility, creativity and patience.

> Other soft skills that are very useful when volunteering are: How do you feel among strangers? Do you establish rapport quickly? Can you take initiative? Can you keep yourself occupied with little or no supervision? How will you deal with culture shock? How will you deal with seeing people in situations much less fortunate than your own?

Knowing what appropriate behavior is in the culture you are visiting will help you establish relationships quickly, and lower the possibility for misunderstandings and frustration on both sides. Learning from books or courses is only a base, because you will still experience culture shock once you are in-country! More about culture and how to prepare for a different cultural experience in paragraph 3.1.

### 1.7.3 Language skills

Speaking Spanish (or Portuguese in Brazil) is paramount to a good volunteer experience in Latin America. There are only a few organizations where you'll be able to communicate effectively in English. We strongly advice against starting your volunteer work without speaking any Spanish (Portuguese). It's not necessary to be fluent, but in the very least you have to be able to have a short, basic conversation that serves as an ice breaker. It would be much better if you could understand detailed instructions on how to perform a task, speak with a community member about his daily life, and discuss differences between your own and your host country. You can imagine that having such conversations will greatly improve the experience you'll be having!

There are two main ways to obtain the language skills needed. 1: you take classes in your home town prior to leaving. Many places have a variety of courses, private classes, local community colleges, etc., where you can take a more or less intensive course. 2: you take intensive language classes upon arrival, before starting your volunteer work. These days, virtually every Latin American town has one or several language schools where you can take an intensive course of 4-8 hours/day in small groups (less than 12 people, often only 4-6) or individual classes at very reasonable rates. These schools always offer lodging options, and can be a perfect way to ease into the experience before taking it one step further and starting with your volunteer work. More on language in paragraph 3.2.

## 1.8 Can I expect compensation?

In the definition of volunteer work that we use in this book we have stated that a volunteer works for 'little or no compensation'.

Many volunteers looking for a position are surprised about the costs involved with volunteering. Many wonder why it's so difficult to find positions that pay for room and board, let alone give you a stipend.

We want to take this opportunity to explain this phenomenon. I think the biggest misconception among volunteers is what room and board really cost. If the project does not have any 'extra' real estate, (and often it doesn't! If it would have more space it would likely use it for the project, right?) then it would have to hire an apartment, shared house or a room in a host family for you. In many cities, there is not much availability for rented real estate, and therefore it's relatively expensive. Or in the larger cities, housing for volunteers must be in the safer, more centrally located, and therefore most expensive areas of the city.

Also, once a project manager commits to renting an apartment for the volunteers, he/she would have to commit for - let's say - 1 year, while his/her volunteers may only be committed to come for a few weeks or a few months at most. So it's likely that at some point, the apartment may be empty while the rent still needs to be paid. Then, you need a stipend to purchase food. If you stay with a host family, the family needs to be compensated for having you. Most families in Latin America do not only host volunteers because of the cultural exchange, but also to generate some extra income. I don't want to imply that they don't enjoy sharing their home, food and culture with volunteers, but I do want to make clear that hosting volunteers can be an important source of income for a family, without which it may be difficult to make ends meet or other solutions would have to be found. For mothers with small children hosting a volunteer could make it possible for her to stay at home and care for her family.

Now, if you calculate how much your lodgings (and meals) cost per month, whether it is in a host family or in a shared apartment, you might be surprised what it amounts up to. In many cases, it's around the level of a local salary.

> So, if the project would have budget for an extra staff member, wouldn't it be best to hire a local person instead of providing foreign volunteers room and board?

The cost of living in many areas of Latin America, as a percentage of the average salary is horrendous. Large families do not only live together because it's their custom, it's an economic necessity. All family members chip in to make ends meet. It's next to impossible to live by yourself or with your partner. This is the very real situation in most so-called 'volunteer hubs' such as Antigua, Guatemala; Quito, Ecuador; Cusco, Peru; and large cities such as Mexico City, Mexico, Sao Paulo, Brazil or Buenos Aires, Argentina.

An exception to this situation can be found in rural areas where you might live in the home of a staff member or project director, or where the compensation for taking you in and giving you room and board is so small that there is a difference between that and a local salary level.

Above paragraphs explained the financial side of providing room and board for volunteers. A second aspect to take into consideration is the <u>time investment the organization needs to make in receiving you</u>. There is a time investment before you arrive: you will send emails, you might need to be picked up from the airport, arrange lodging, etc. Then, when you arrive, everybody needs to get to know you, you need to be shown around and your tasks need to be explained to you. And since they don't know you, it's a gamble to see if you fit in the team and really be able to help out as promised. Nobody thinks you won't, but it's a fact that the project members do not know you before you arrive. Getting you up and running, and thus useful for the project, requires a time investment.

This time cannot be spent on other tasks. So if you only have 2 weeks time, how much use is that for the organization? Put yourself in their place and think honestly if you think it's a smart idea to give every volunteer room and board in an expensive city even if he/she stays for a few weeks….. Probably not, right?

> You may say: "I am a social worker with 15 years of experience working with street children, my Spanish is fluent and I can stay for 3 months" Well, then….. that changes things, doesn't it? In that case I can guarantee you that you will find an organization that would be so happy if you want to come help them out that they will make a concerted effort to help you with your expenses while in-country. And if the first project you contact doesn't provide this, I can guarantee you that there will be other projects that will!

Concluding, there are volunteer positions where you'll receive room and board, but they are much harder to find, and organizations tend to ask for more in return. So if you are willing to commit for a longer period of time, speak Spanish (or Portuguese) at a high level, have specific, in-demand skills, etc., it makes it more worthwhile for the project to invest in you. If you cannot meet these requirements we hope that the above explanation helps you understand better (and therefore not feel bad or exploited) if an organization cannot offer you room and board.

## 1.9 Long-term vs. short-term volunteering

As mentioned in the above paragraph, there are many people looking for very short-term commitments, and we need to be aware that meeting new volunteers, showing them around and making them familiar with the tasks does require a time investment from the staff at the volunteer project. I think it's extremely important to realize not only what you want to get out of your experience, but also to think realistically about what your presence contributes to the organization. You can imagine that the longer you are with an organization the more you can contribute to the organization's goal. If you can commit for 6 months you will see that you have immediately become a very attractive candidate, even if you are not skilled in the type of work you're looking to do!

The reality of life is that many people do not have the luxury to commit to performing unpaid work for such long periods. Short-term volunteering is often the only possibility, and then we speak from experience if we say that it's always better to do a short program than to miss out on the experience! Did you know that there are possibilities to combine multiple short-term programs for a rich, full, cultural experience of Latin America? You can also make it an interesting stopping point on a long round-the-world trip.

The advantages of long-term commitment are:
* You learn more and you can contribute in a more lasting way;
* Sometimes room & board are provided;
* You'll have time to form a deeper connection with the organization;
* You'll learn much more about the culture;
* You have more time to form local friendships.

We recommend that you find a happy balance. <u>Commit for the longest time that you're absolutely sure of</u>. We don't recommend that you sign up for a long commitment if you're not reasonably sure you'll honor it, as letting the organization down can really hurt the work they are trying to do, not to speak of the effect this will have on any future potential volunteers. Often, receiving organizations and/or intermediaries have a clause in their terms and conditions that if you cut your commitment short you will not be refunded the costs for room and board (if applicable) that you have paid. These stipulations are not meant to make money, they are only meant as a strong motivator not to break your commitment.

## 1.10 Matching the volunteer work with your needs

Now you know a bit more about which options for volunteer work exist and how receiving organizations view volunteer work, it's time for you to decide what your mayor goals for the experience are.

It is important that you've read the paragraphs about reasons for volunteering, skill sets and why organizations receive volunteers before you do the exercises below.

**First:** you need to ask yourself 'What do you want to achieve?' Go back to paragraph 1.3, and after re-reading the paragraph make your own list. Then, think about which type of work or which type of organization is most likely to provide you with the opportunities to fulfill these goals.

1. Altruistic reasons:

..............................................................................
..............................................................................
..............................................................................
..............................................................................
..............................................................................
..............................................................................
..............................................................................
..............................................................................
..............................................................................
..............................................................................

2. Personal reasons:

..............................................................................
..............................................................................
..............................................................................
..............................................................................
..............................................................................
..............................................................................
..............................................................................
..............................................................................
..............................................................................
..............................................................................
..............................................................................

**Second:** take stock of what you have to offer to the type of organization of your choice. Why would they take you? Try to think beyond the skills you would list on your resume and put yourself in the shoes of the receiving organization. What do they need?

1. Professional skills: Work experience, Life experience, Education, Hobbies

..............................................................................
..............................................................................
..............................................................................
..............................................................................
..............................................................................
..............................................................................
..............................................................................
..............................................................................
..............................................................................
..............................................................................

2. Soft skills: Experience volunteering, experience living/working in Latin America

..............................................................................
..............................................................................
..............................................................................
..............................................................................
..............................................................................
..............................................................................
..............................................................................
..............................................................................
..............................................................................
..............................................................................
..............................................................................

3. Language skills: What level is your Spanish/Portuguese? How is your spoken, written and oral level? Are you familiar with the accent and colloquialism of the country you're interested in?

..................................................................................
..................................................................................
..................................................................................
..................................................................................
..................................................................................
..................................................................................
..................................................................................
..................................................................................
..................................................................................
..................................................................................
..................................................................................

**Third:** make a list of the practical aspects of your volunteering adventure. Think about the following aspects:

1. Available time. How long can I volunteer?
..................................................................

2. Can I work fulltime or part-time?
..................................................................................

3. Available funds; How much money do I have? Can I trade time for funds (for example by committing for a year's volunteering to receive free room and board)? Shall I choose a region which has a lower cost of living (you can imagine that life in Rio de Janeiro is more expensive than in La Ceiba, Honduras)? Can I choose a region that is cheaper to fly to (flying to Cancun,

Mexico is much cheaper than to Merida, Venezuela)?
..............................................................................
..............................................................................
..............................................................................

4. Am I willing to pay an agency or intermediary to help me organize my volunteer work? (more information on this in chapter 2)
..............................................................................

5. Am I willing to pay an enrollment fee or obligatory donation to the organization where I will volunteer? If so, how much?
..............................................................................

6. Do I have environmental allergies that influence where I can live and work?
..............................................................................
..............................................................................
..............................................................................
..............................................................................

7. Do I have dietary requirements or illnesses that influence where I can live and work?
..............................................................................
..............................................................................
..............................................................................
..............................................................................

8. Where do I feel most comfortable? In a big city, town or rural environment?
..............................................................................
..............................................................................
..............................................................................

9. Do I need modern conveniences such as reliable electricity and movie theaters or am I also comfortable in places where the electricity supply is erratic and where I cannot flush my toilet paper?
..................................................................................
..................................................................................

10. Do I want to be in contact with other international volunteers or be the only foreigner?
..................................................................................
..................................................................................

11. Can I work in a fully Spanish/Portuguese speaking environment or do I prefer that there is at least 1 person who speaks English (or your native tongue)?
..................................................................................
..................................................................................

12. Do I want to live with a host family, in a private or shared apartment?
..................................................................................
..................................................................................

13. What climate suits me best?
..................................................................................
..................................................................................

This exercise is all about finding out what you want and what –realistically speaking- your options are. Once you have your list complete, you can use the Latin American volunteer destination guide as a reference to have an idea where you can find the ideal environment for you to volunteer in.

## 1.11 Latin American Volunteer destination guide

For you to have a fantastic, fun and rewarding volunteer experience, you need to live in a place where you feel comfortable. There is no best destination for volunteer work, but there certainly is a best destination for you!

To help you find out which country and place is best for you, we have ranked each country (and sometimes have we distinguished different areas within a country) on all aspects that influence your volunteer experience.

Using the explanations below and the volunteer destination guide that you'll find at the end of this section, make a top 3 or top 5 list of destinations. Then, find out more about these areas by doing research on the internet, reading guide books and by talking to people who have been there. Once you've narrowed your options down to 2 or maximum 3 destinations, start looking for specific projects using the information we will give you in the following chapters.

We have ranked all Latin American countries on 27 aspects. For most items we have used a star (*) system, where more stars mean more/higher scores. Below you find an explanation about each aspect:

1. Costs of living and travel: 1 star means very cheap; and 5-star countries are the most expensive in Latin America. This is a relative ranking; even the 5-star destinations in Latin America are cheaper than most Western countries.

2. Accommodation options: here only the <u>amount</u> and <u>variety</u> of options is ranked, not their comfort level. If a destination received 1 star, this means that there usually is only 1 type of accommodation to choose from. 5 stars mean a wide variety of accommodation types (for example; host family, shared apartments, private apartments, dorm rooms with meals, and hotels) and usually different price/ comfort level options within each type.

3. Average cost of lodging: 1 star mean very cheap; 5 stars mean relatively expensive.

4. Costs of international plane tickets: Again, the stars give an indication from (relatively) the cheapest to the most expensive destinations. Please note that the indications in this aspect are very general, as it depends mostly on where you are coming from. Flights from Australia to South America tend to be cheaper then if you were coming from North America, for example. Also, flying from North America to Mexico is cheaper than flying to Brazil, whereas from Europe, the prices are comparable. Use these indications as a starting point but <u>do your own research</u> before deciding on a destination.

5. Cheapest tickets available in: As you know, flight prices vary significantly throughout the year. Traveling in low season or buying far (months) in advance can save more than 50% in most cases. Adjusting your travel schedule can allow you to stay months longer in your chosen destination.

6. **Prevalence of high enrollment fees or obligatory donation:** As discussed in chapter 1.6, some organizations require you to pay a fee to be allowed to volunteer there. This topic rates the likelihood of encountering such organizations. We could do this because often when local projects see that other projects in the same town get away with this, they start doing it too. 1 star means not many organizations charge high fees, 5 stars that it is very likely that the volunteer organization of your choice charges money for volunteering. Note; this is not the same for agencies or intermediaries charging a fee for their services. This topic refers to the receiving volunteer projects themselves charging fees (they may call it donation) without giving any services in return.

7. **Most common types of volunteer work:** States which types of volunteer work are most common. This doesn't mean you can't find other types of work!

8. **Is it easy to find volunteer work for un- and low skilled volunteers?:** 1 star mean that is it very difficult to find volunteer work for un- and low-skilled volunteers, and 5 stars mean it is very easy.

9. **Are communities and projects used to receiving volunteers?:** 1 star means that the community or organizations in that area are not very used to receiving international volunteers; 5 stars mean that they are very used to it.

10. **Presence of other volunteers;** 1 star means very few volunteers; 5 stars means a large community of foreign volunteers.

11. Probability of compensated (stipend or room & board) volunteer work: 1 star means it's near to impossible, while 5 stars mean that it is fairly easy to find such a project. Don't forget that compensation usually mean that you have to commit for several months (at least 3-6 months) and/or have to have specific skills.

12. Probability of finding paid work: 1 star means that it's not likely at all, 5 stars mean that it is do-able. You have to understand that 'paid work' in this context means receiving a local salary, usually just a few US dollars per day. Most of the paid work that foreigners find in Latin America is working in a bar/restaurant or teaching English.

13. Governmental rules & regulations for volunteering (i.e. visa needed): 1 star means that it is easy; you can perform volunteer work on a tourist visa (as long as you don't get compensation! See chapter ¡Error!No se encuentra el origen de la referencia.) while 5-stars mean that most nationalities have to apply for a visa in advance and that governments have strict rules governing volunteer work and will reinforce them. Always contact the consulate of the country of your choice before you make any decisions. Rules & regulations vary per country and can change frequently!

14. Restrictions for volunteering (especially in the health care field): Often, there is a difference between volunteering in most organizations and volunteering in health care. Direct patient contact can be more or less restricted (and reinforced) by government. 1 star means few restrictions, 5 stars means many

restrictions. In the last situation, you have to expect not to be able to have any direct patient contact if you're not a licensed professional in that country. Shadowing is probably all you will be able to do.

15. Variety of food/ access to non-standard food (such as soy milk, vegetarian options). 1 star means that food in general is not very varied and that dietary products or specialty food (meaning not common in that country) are not available. 5 stars mean that there is easy access to a large variety of different food types, cuisines and that you can find specialty food.

16. Availability of historical sights: 1 star means few to none historical sights within a day-trip's distance, while 5 stars mean many and/or world famous sights within easy travel distance.

17. Availability of natural sights: 1 star means little to no nature within a day-trip's distance, while 5 stars mean many different and/or world renowned natural sights within easy travel distance.

18. Availability of (modern) culture, gastronomy, arts: 1 star means little to none; 5 stars mean many different cultural offerings.

19. Entertainment options: 1 star means little to none; 5 stars mean many different offerings. For every budget and preference there are several options.

20. Reliability of electricity, water, modern plumbing: While virtually all projects have running water,

electricity and some plumbing, it may not be available 24 hours a day or it may be very unreliable, meaning that you run the risk to have to do without the commodity for days on end. When a destination scores 1 star this is very likely to happen; when a destination received 5 stars the level and reliability of service is (nearly) equal to Western countries. Note that when you stay in more expensive accommodation, you can expect the service level of the amenities to be higher than average for that destination.

21. Presence of high quality hospitals: 1 star means there is no hospital with Western levels of care within easy traveling distance; 5 stars mean that there are several hospitals (always private) where you receive care to the highest international standards. Many of the physicians will have trained in US or European hospitals/ universities. 3 stars mean that there is a good, private hospital within easy traveling distance.

22. Presence of environmental allergens; This is difficult to value, as different people are allergic to different things. Generally, 1 star means little natural allergens (such as pollen) and little air pollution (often at higher altitudes with dry air). 3 stars mean average conditions for most patients; and 5 stars mean polluted air and/ or many natural allergens (think tropical rain forest and large polluted cities). If you suffer from allergies, please research the presence of your allergens in your top 5 destinations before making a final choice.

23. Presence of English speakers: 1 star means that you probably won't find any English speakers; 5 stars mean that there are many.

 24. Safety: 1 star means that the country is not very safe. That doesn't mean you should not travel there, but it does mean you need to take precautions (see chapter 3.6.). 5 stars means that you are as safe as you would be in a medium-sized town in an average Western country (which still means you shouldn't be leaving your belongings about!).

 25. Health hazards: 1 star means few health hazards; comparable with a Western country. 5 stars means you are almost guaranteed to contract something, most likely 'Montezuma's revenge' (see chapter 3.5).

 26. Language spoken: This notes (one of) the official languages of the country. In many Latin American countries there are large indigenous groups who speak their own language, which may or may not be recognized as an official language in that country. You may end up volunteering in an area where Spanish (or Portuguese) is most people's second language!

 27. Climate: A general description of the climate in the country and mayor volunteer hubs of your choice. Before making a final decision, research the climate in the area where you will be living.

| | |
|---|---|
| 1 | Cost of living & travel |
| 2 | Accommodation options |
| 3 | Average cost of lodging |
| 4 | Cost of international plane tickets |
| 5 | Cheapest tickets available in |
| 6 | Prevalence of high enrollment fees or obligatory donations |
| 7 | Most common types of volunteer work |
| 8 | Is it easy to find vol. work for un- and low skilled volunteers? |
| 9 | Are communities and projects used to receiving volunteers? |
| 10 | Presence of other volunteers |
| 11 | Probability of finding compensated volunteer work |
| 12 | Probability of finding paid work |
| 13 | Governmental regulations for volunteering (i.e. visa needed) |
| 14 | Restrictions for volunteering (especially health care field) |
| 15 | Variety of food/ access to non-standard food |
| 16 | Availability of historical sights |
| 17 | Availability of natural sights |
| 18 | Availability of (modern) culture, gastronomy, arts |
| 19 | Entertainment options |
| 20 | Reliability of electricity, water, modern plumbing |
| 21 | Presence of high quality hospitals |
| 22 | Presence of environmental allergens |
| 23 | Presence of English speakers |
| 24 | Safety |
| 25 | Health hazards |
| 26 | Language spoken |
| 27 | Climate |

| Argentina | Buenos Aires | Cordoba | |
|---|---|---|---|
| **** | ***** | **** | 1 |
| *** | ***** | ***** | 2 |
| ***** | ***** | **** | 3 |
| *** | *** | **** | 4 |
| March-June + Sept-Nov | March-June + Sept-Nov | March-June + Sept-Nov | 5 |
| ** | ** | ** | 6 |
| Social, Internships | Social, Internships | Social, Internships | 7 |
| ** | ** | ** | 8 |
| Yes | Yes | Yes | 9 |
| * | * | * | 10 |
| ** | ** | ** | 11 |
| *** | *** | *** | 12 |
| * | | | 13 |
| *** | | | 14 |
| ** | ** | ** | 15 |
| ** | ** | ** | 16 |
| ***** | * | ** | 17 |
| **** | ***** | **** | 18 |
| *** | ***** | **** | 19 |
| ***** | ***** | ***** | 20 |
| *** | ***** | **** | 21 |
| **** | ** | ** | 22 |
| ** | *** | *** | 23 |
| **** | ** | *** | 24 |
| * | * | * | 25 |
| Spanish | Spanish | Spanish | 26 |
| Very varied; from high altitude desert in the North, Tropical in the North-East to Sub-antarctic in the South. In middle: 4 distinct seasons - opposite to Northern hemisphere | | | 27 |

|    | Belize | Bolivia | Cochabamba |
|----|--------|---------|------------|
| 1  | ** | * | * |
| 2  | * | * | * |
| 3  | ** | * | * |
| 4  | ** | *** | ***** |
| 5  | Sep-Nov + Feb-Jun | October-April | October-April |
| 6  | *** | *** | *** |
| 7  | Nature conservancy | Social, Healthcare | Social, Healthcare |
| 8  | ***** | *** | *** |
| 9  | Yes | Yes | Yes |
| 10 | **** | *** | *** |
| 11 | * | ** | ** |
| 12 | * | * | * |
| 13 | * | ** (US citizens; | |
| 14 | ** | *** | |
| 15 | ** | * | * |
| 16 | **** | *** | *** |
| 17 | *** | **** | *** |
| 18 | ** | ** | ** |
| 19 | * | * | * |
| 20 | ** | * | ** |
| 21 | ** | * | * |
| 22 | ***** | * | * |
| 23 | ***** | * | * |
| 24 | *** | ** | ** |
| 25 | **** | **** | *** |
| 26 | English | Spanish | Spanish |
| 27 | Dry season: Dec-May; Rainy season: Jun-Nov | Highlands: Strong variations between night&day; Lowlands: hot in dry season, hot&humid in rainy season | |

| La Paz | Sucre | Brazil | |
|---|---|---|---|
| * | ** | **** | 1 |
| * | * | ** | 2 |
| * | ** | ** | 3 |
| *** | ***** | * | 4 |
| October-April | October-April | March-June + August-October | 5 |
| ** | *** | * | 6 |
| Social, Healthcare | Social, Healthcare | Social | 7 |
| ** | *** | *** | 8 |
| Yes | Yes | ** | 9 |
| ** | *** | * | 10 |
| ** | ** | ** | 11 |
| * | * | ** | 12 |
| | | **** | 13 |
| | | ** | 14 |
| * | * | *** | 15 |
| *** | *** | *** | 16 |
| ** | *** | **** | 17 |
| ** | ** | **** | 18 |
| ** | ** | *** | 19 |
| ** | ** | *** | 20 |
| *** | * | ** | 21 |
| ** | * | ***** | 22 |
| * | ** | ** | 23 |
| * | ** | ** | 24 |
| *** | *** | *** | 25 |
| Spanish | Spanish | Portuguese | 26 |
| | | Subropical in North and Amazonia; More defined seasons further South | 27 |

|    | Rio de Janeiro | Sao Paulo | Chile |
|----|---|---|---|
| 1  | ***** | ***** | **** |
| 2  | ** | ** | ** |
| 3  | ** | ** | **** |
| 4  | ** | * | *** |
| 5  | March-June + August-October | March-June + August-October | March-Nov |
| 6  | * | * | ** |
| 7  | Social | Social | Social |
| 8  | *** | *** | ** |
| 9  | ** | ** | * |
| 10 | * | * | * |
| 11 | ** | ** | ** |
| 12 | *** | *** | ** |
| 13 |   |   | ** |
| 14 |   |   | *** |
| 15 | ***** | ***** | ** |
| 16 | *** | *** | *** |
| 17 | ** | ** | ***** |
| 18 | **** | **** | **** |
| 19 | ***** | ***** | *** |
| 20 | **** | **** | *** |
| 21 | ***** | ***** | *** |
| 22 | *** | *** | ** |
| 23 | *** | *** | ** |
| 24 | * | * | **** |
| 25 | ** | ** | ** |
| 26 | Portuguese | Portuguese | Spanish |
| 27 |   |   | From high altitude desert (warm during the day, freezing at night) to moderate in Santiago and cool in the South |

# 1 • Why working as a volunteer?

| Santiago | Costa Rica | Valle Central | |
|---|---|---|---|
| ***** | *** | **** | 1 |
| **** | ** | **** | 2 |
| ***** | *** | ** | 3 |
| *** | ** | ** | 4 |
| March-Nov | Sep-Nov + Mar-Jun | Sep-Nov + Mar-Jun | 5 |
| ** | **** | *** | 6 |
| Social, Internships | Nature convervancy | Social, Healthcare | 7 |
| ** | ***** | *** | 8 |
| * | ***** | **** | 9 |
| * | ***** | *** | 10 |
| ** | ** | ** | 11 |
| ** | * | * | 12 |
| | * | | 13 |
| | ** | | 14 |
| *** | ** | *** | 15 |
| *** | ** | *** | 16 |
| ***** | **** | *** | 17 |
| **** | * | ** | 18 |
| ***** | * | *** | 19 |
| **** | ** | *** | 20 |
| **** | * | *** | 21 |
| *** | ***** | **** | 22 |
| *** | ** | *** | 23 |
| ** | *** | *** | 24 |
| ** | **** | *** | 25 |
| Spanish | Spanish | Spanish | 26 |
| | Tropical; warm in dry season (Dec-Apr); hot and humid in rainy season (May-Nov) | | 27 |

| | Guatemala | Antigua | Ecuador |
|---|---|---|---|
| 1 | * | * | *** |
| 2 | ** | **** | ** |
| 3 | * | ** | ** |
| 4 | ** | ** | *** |
| 5 | Sep-Nov + Feb-Jun | Sep-Nov + Feb-Jun | Jan-Jun + Oct-Nov |
| 6 | **** | **** | ** |
| 7 | Social | Social | Social, Nature conservancy |
| 8 | *** | *** | ** |
| 9 | **** | **** | ** |
| 10 | *** | ***** | ** |
| 11 | ** | * | ** |
| 12 | * | ** | * |
| 13 | * | | ** |
| 14 | * | | *** |
| 15 | * | *** | * |
| 16 | ***** | ***** | *** |
| 17 | ***** | ***** | **** |
| 18 | * | ** | ** |
| 19 | * | ** | * |
| 20 | * | ** | * |
| 21 | * | *** | * |
| 22 | * | ** | **** |
| 23 | * | *** | * |
| 24 | * | ** | ** |
| 25 | ***** | *** | **** |
| 26 | Spanish | Spanish | Spanish |
| 27 | Tropical; warm in dry season (Nov-Apr); hot and humid in rainy season (May-Oct); more moderate in higher elevations | | Highlands: pleasant temperatures year-round; Amazon and Galapagos: hot & humid Jan-April, rest of year warm and dry; |

# 1 • Why working as a volunteer?

| Quito | El Salvador | Honduras | |
|---|---|---|---|
| *** | * | * | 1 |
| **** | * | * | 2 |
| ** | * | * | 3 |
| *** | ** | ** | 4 |
| Jan-Jun + Oct-Nov | Sep-May | Sep-May | 5 |
| ** | * | ** | 6 |
| Social | Social | Social | 7 |
| ** | * | ** | 8 |
| ** | * | * | 9 |
| ** | * | * | 10 |
| ** | * | * | 11 |
| ** | * | * | 12 |
| | ** | ** | 13 |
| | ** | ** | 14 |
| *** | * | ** | 15 |
| *** | * | *** | 16 |
| ** | * | **** | 17 |
| *** | * | * | 18 |
| *** | * | * | 19 |
| *** | * | * | 20 |
| **** | ** | * | 21 |
| ** | **** | **** | 22 |
| ** | * | * | 23 |
| ** | * | | 24 |
| ** | **** | | 25 |
| Spanish | Spanish | Spanish | 26 |
| | Tropical; warm in dry season (Nov-Apr); hot and humid in rainy season (May-Oct) | Tropical; warm in dry season (Nov-Apr); hot and humid in rainy season (May-Oct) | 27 |

|    | Nicaragua | Granada | Mexico |
|----|-----------|---------|--------|
| 1  | * | ** | *** |
| 2  | * | *** | ** |
| 3  | * | ** | *** |
| 4  | ** | ** | * |
| 5  | Sep-May | Sep-May | Sep-Nov + Mar-May |
| 6  | ** | ** | ** |
| 7  | Social, Nature conservancy | Social | Social, Internships, Nature |
| 8  | ** | ** | ** |
| 9  | ** | ** | *** |
| 10 | * | ** | ** |
| 11 | * | * | *** |
| 12 | * | * | ** |
| 13 | ** |   | *** |
| 14 | * |   | ** |
| 15 | * | ** | ***** |
| 16 | ** | *** | ***** |
| 17 | **** | *** | ***** |
| 18 | * | ** | ** |
| 19 | * | *** | ** |
| 20 | * | ** | **** |
| 21 | * | ** | *** |
| 22 | **** | **** | *** |
| 23 | * | ** | *** |
| 24 |   |   |   |
| 25 |   |   |   |
| 26 | Spanish | Spanish | Spanish |
| 27 | Tropical; warm in dry season (Nov-Apr); hot and humid in rainy season (May-Oct) |   | Very varied; from desert in the North, Tropical in the Yucatan to Sub-tropical in the middle states. Hurricanes occur in the summer and fall |

# 1 • Why working as a volunteer?

| Panama | Peru | Cusco | |
|---|---|---|---|
| *** | ** | *** | 1 |
| * | ** | *** | 2 |
| *** | *** | *** | 3 |
| ** | **** | ***** | 4 |
| Sep-Nov + Mar-Jun | Feb-Jun + Sep-Nov | | 5 |
| *** | **** | **** | 6 |
| Nature conservancy, Social | Social | Social | 7 |
| * | *** | ** | 8 |
| ** | *** | **** | 9 |
| *** | *** | **** | 10 |
| * | ** | * | 11 |
| ** | * | * | 12 |
| * | * | | 13 |
| ** | *** | | 14 |
| * | * | **** | 15 |
| ** | ***** | ***** | 16 |
| *** | **** | *** | 17 |
| ** | * | *** | 18 |
| * | * | ** | 19 |
| *** | * | ** | 20 |
| *** | * | ** | 21 |
| **** | *** | ** | 22 |
| ** | * | ** | 23 |
| *** | ** | ** | 24 |
| **** | **** | *** | 25 |
| Spanish | Spanish | Spanish | 26 |
| Tropical; warm in dry season (Jan-Mar); hot and humid in rainy season (Apr-Dec) | Lima: warm in summer, cool in winter; Andes; moderate in summer and cold in winter; Jungle; warm and humid year-round | | 27 |

|    | Venezuela | Uruguay |
|----|-----------|---------|
| 1  | ** | **** |
| 2  | * | *** |
| 3  | ** | **** |
| 4  | * | **** |
| 5  | Not much variation troughout the year | Mar-June + Sep-Nov |
| 6  | * | ** |
| 7  | Social, Nature conservancy | Social |
| 8  | ** | ** |
| 9  | * | * |
| 10 | * | * |
| 11 | ** | ** |
| 12 | * | ** |
| 13 | * | * |
| 14 | * | * |
| 15 | ** | ** |
| 16 | ** | ** |
| 17 | **** | ** |
| 18 | * | *** |
| 19 | ** | *** |
| 20 | * | **** |
| 21 | *** | **** |
| 22 | **** | *** |
| 23 | * | * |
| 24 | ** | **** |
| 25 | **** | ** |
| 26 | Spanish | Spanish |
| 27 | Tropical, with dry season (Nov-May) and rainy season (June-Oct). Moderate in mountaneous areas | Temperate, with 4 distinct seasons; those are reverse to those in the Northern hemisphere |

# 2

## Finding a Volunteer position

If you've read the first chapter and you have done all the exercises, you should have a pretty clear idea about what type of volunteer work you want to do, how long you want to volunteer for, and you have your top 3 list of places where you would like to go. Now you can start the search for the actual project!

There are three ways you can go about your search;

1. You can use the services of a travel agency or intermediary in your country. Every country has travel agencies that are specialized in arranging for volunteer experiences abroad. Either 'alternative' (adventure, responsible) travel agencies or travel agencies focused on young people and students should be able to help you.

2. You can also enlist the services of a coordinator or intermediary in the country where you want to volunteer.

3. Lastly, you can forgo any intermediaries and contact the organization you would like to work for directly. Each option has advantages and disadvantages and there is no one best option that works for everyone. You need to find out what works for you. In the following paragraphs each of these options are discussed in detail, also giving you lists of trusted agencies, intermediaries and organizations.

## 2.1 Through Agencies/ Intermediaries

In this chapter we will explain what an agency is and what you can expect from one. We will also give you and idea what these services cost and how you can evaluate if an agency can provide you what you need. Lastly, this paragraph contains a list of trusted agencies in various countries, to give you a starting point, and tips on applying if you decide to use this route.

### 2.1.1 What is an agency or intermediary?

An agency is an organization that organizes volunteer experiences for individuals who (usually) live in the same country as where the agency is located. You will have to submit your application with the agency and they will take care of everything. The agency is your point of contact for all questions and concerns.

### 2.1.2 How do agencies/ intermediaries work

If you look at organizing volunteer experiences as a business, which an agency obviously does (and needs to do!), you can split the activities in two parts. One is the business of selling volunteer programs. How do you convince individuals to embark on a volunteer adventure and more specifically, how do you convince them to use your organization to organize the program for you? This requires Marketing, Communication, PR and Sales experts. These are the people that think about which information you want to have and in which format you want to see it. They make the glossy brochures and organize information fairs. They also influence to an extent the look & feel of all information that you receive once you are their client. In the end, you pay their salaries. This is simply how things work. You also pay for the t-shirts of your favorite football team, the swanky cola-cola commercials and the manager of your favorite band. There is no such thing as a free lunch.

The other set of activities an agency engages in, is the communication with Latin America. The agency will almost always have a partner in Latin America who takes care of the in-country logistics. Most often, there will be one contact per country the agency offers programs in. This means that the agency does not have direct contact with the people at the volunteer projects. Reputable agencies do have a very close and frank relationship with the in-country contacts, and will send their staff regularly to Latin America to visit projects. Over the years, they will have personally visited almost all projects they offer to their clients. The in-country contact is extremely important for the agency, as this organization knows (or should know) all the organizations that receive volunteers. Usually it's the in-country contact that matches the volunteers with individual projects.

The in-country contact also takes care of:
- Airport pickups;
- Arranging language classes;
- Arranging accommodation (if necessary);
- Double-checking with the receiving organization if they haven't forgotten about the arriving volunteer.

The in-country contact further also:
- Supports the volunteer during his/her experience;
- Takes the volunteer to the project;
- Gives instructions about cultural differences;
- Supports the volunteer in his/her cultural adaptation process;
- Answers questions about the volunteer project;
- Mediates in case of problem or misunderstandings;
- and generally act as the confidant of the volunteer.

Yes, you pay for this person (or organization) too!
The agency makes the switch, or translation, between the way

things are run in the countries where they offer volunteer programs, and the way the client likes to see things. With 'translation' we don't mean literal translation (even though that is often an important task too!) but cultural translation.

The in-country contact is usually an organization or person with reasonable to good English speaking skills, and with a lot of experience interacting with foreigners. That said, normally the person is Latin American. Latino's have a more high-context style of communicating, are less concerned with deadlines and details and prefer spontaneous adaptation to careful advance planning.

Most Anglo-Saxon and all Germanic cultures are precisely the opposite in these aspects and you can imagine that this can be a recipe for disaster. Especially when we get a little nervous- and almost everybody is when leaving for a long period of time to work in a new country – in those circumstances you revert stronger to your natural cultural tendencies. So when they don't get satisfied, you might get even more nervous!

Precisely this is the biggest added value of the agency or intermediary. They make sure you receive the information in the format you like to receive it, in your own language, according to your own cultural rules, in a time where you'll be dealing with a lot of nerve-wrecking details.

## 2.1.3 What can you expect from an agency/ intermediary

- You can expect that an agency knows its clients' needs and has developed a program that matches your needs and present information in a format you feel comfortable with.

- You can expect your agency to have a contact in each country they are active in who will act as a liaison between you and the organization you are going to work at. In case of conflict you have someone in your corner, so to speak.

- You can expect your agency to provide you with lots of practical information in your own language.

- You can expect that the in-country contact your agency works with speaks at least fluent English.

- You can expect that your agency has ample knowledge of the advantages and disadvantages of each destination and each type of volunteer project, and can advice you which type of work and which setting will best suit your needs.

- You can expect your agency to arrange your flight (sometimes optional), airport pickup, accommodation from the beginning (you may need 1 night accommodation close to the airport before traveling to your final destination), language classes if necessary, an introduction to the organization and continued support (as needed) while working on the project.

- Further, you should be able to contact the agency for advice on what to bring, health care, insurance, travel after volunteering, put you into contact with other volunteers through the same organization who will be there at the same time, etc.

## 2.1.4 Advantages/ Disadvantages

**Advantage**: Excellent level and range of services

1. Communication in your language and culture;

2. Help with visa applications if necessary;

3. Using an agency will save you a lot of time. You don't have to re-invent the wheel;

4. The agencies' staff is highly experienced in matching candidates with projects, and is usually very good at advising you on your options;

5. Agencies in your own country are usually members of professional organizations, giving you financial and quality guarantees;

6. Up-to-date information on the local situation on vaccinations, health precautions and insurance options;

7. If reputable, the organization will have carefully selected the best partners and projects for a reasonable price;

8. Often, agencies will have contacts with organizations that do not receive volunteers directly (or do not advertise that fact anywhere);

9. If the agency sends many volunteers to an in-country partner and/or a hosting organization it has a lot of influencing power to make sure your experience lives up to expectations, this is especially important when you're unhappy and you want to

make changes;

10. Most agencies have an emergency contact number that you and your family can call 24/7.

**Disadvantages**: The main disadvantage is higher costs and adding another 'layer' between you and your volunteer project
1. Costs;

2. No direct contact with hosting organization; possible loss of information at each 'intermediary station' (from you to volunteer project and vice versa);

3. You usually can't choose the precise organization you are going to work for – this will be decided for you based on the information you provided on your application;

4. Sometimes (not always) no possibilities for compensated (room & board provided) options.

## 2.1.5 Costs/ Cost structure

The amount of money you pay to an agency consists of several elements; first, the basic elements of volunteering that you'll pay for anyway: Accommodation; Meals (if included) and Transportation (if included).

Then you'll pay for the in-country contact, usually a flat fee which often also includes an amount that will be used for donations to the various projects an organization works with.

Lastly, you pay for the services your agency provides you (security, knowledge, preparation, cultural and linguistic preparation, guarantees, support, logistical assistance).

We don't care how these elements are brought together in the final pricing -it may be one round fee or you may pay an enrollment fee on top of your accommodation and meal cost – that is irrelevant. In the end these are the costs that have to be offset.

An agency can also help you save money by arranging discounts on airfare, transportation, insurance and/or language courses.

In this section it's useful to say something about non-profit vs, for-profit volunteer agencies. Being non-profit does not equal 'cheaper' nor 'more benefits for Latin America'. Non-profit does not mean cheap, as overhead (including salaries of staff members and managers/ directors) are costs not profit. I know of large organizations that run their volunteer agency services at-cost or at a loss, as they use profit from other programs to pay for the resources (i.e. staff) of the volunteer program. It fits in their philosophy of supporting communities in Latin America. Wonderful and why wouldn't you enjoy that benefit? See the separate box on this page for more details on this topic.

> Non-profit volunteer organizations are a special story. In our opinion, the majority of the non-profit organizations are truly non-profit, but others merely trade on the good image of non-profit. Non-profit only means that the organization does not make a profit. It does not mean that the people working there don't make a good income or that the organization is smart about spending money. You can be an owner of a non-profit organization

and make yourself CEO or Director, with a 'market conform' salary. That's fine, no problems with that. You have to live, right? We just want to make you think about what the difference is between this person and the owner of the for-profit organization who works just as hard, doesn't pay him/herself a salary but pulls out a certain amount of the profits to live on. In numbers, it's likely the same (or not so much when investments are needed or market conditions are tough). This example is just to illustrate that appearances can be deceiving and you need to look a little further than first glance. You can easily find programs at non-profit organizations that are as expensive as those at for-profit organizations – so where's the benefit then? Look into (or search on the Internet) for published financial reports of volunteer organizations and look how much of the revenue is used in the country where the organization is situated, and how much of the revenue ends up with the partners in Latin America. Someone who runs an organization with a 80% overhead is in our eyes not a very convincing altruist. Unfortunately, I have seen organizations which are set up like this and one of the reasons to write this book is to educate prospective volunteers in the business of volunteering and help them make informed choices. Nobody is in the volunteer business to get wealthy, not the non-profits nor the for-profits. But we don't like organizations that pretend to support development in Latin America but don't actually divert a lot of revenue to that continent.

## 2.1.6 Evaluating agencies/intermediaries

How do you know that an agency is providing you with the level of services you need? You need to find a partner that provides not more but certainly not less of the services that you require. An intermediary inevitably will have to get paid for its efforts. Of course, part of these costs can be offset by savings the intermediary can arrange for you, for example discounts on lodging, airfare, other transportation or language courses.

Consider the language barrier; if you are interested in working with a locally-run organization, you will need to communicate in Spanish (or Portuguese if you want to go to Brazil). If your Spanish/Portuguese is not good enough for detailed communication, this could be a good reason to enlist the help of an agency.

Don't limit yourself to agencies in your area or country – maybe an agency located further away or in another country provides you with exactly what you need. Do bear in mind that if you will be needing a visa then sometimes you are obligated to work with an intermediary in your own country.

Ask questions! All agencies are different. Some are specialized in a certain geographical area, others in a type of program, some have clearly defined programs and others are more flexible. Thoroughly research what you need and don't be afraid to contact several agencies, stating your plans and asking them how they can help you.

A good organization doesn't mean it's good for everybody. Go back to your list of needs and compare that to the conditions offered by the volunteer organization. Is this what you are looking for? Where are the discrepancies? Can you live with that? It's important to realize that above all, you'll need flexibility to enjoy your volunteer experience in Latin America. However, it will be much easier for you to be flexible on minor points if you have those aspects of the experience that are most important to you, organized to your preference. Think about climate, immediate environment (rural, village, town, cosmopolitan city), living options and conditions, availability, pricing and safety of food, distance to your work and how you'll get there (walking, public transportation), working hours, free time, language, presence of people your age, presence of other volunteers or travelers.

Many agencies will organize information days, be present at study/work/work experience fairs or even specific volunteer abroad fairs. This is a great way of personally meeting the people behind the organization and see if there is a match in outlook and way of working.

Verify if the organization of your choice is a member of professional associations providing you with guarantees.

## 2.1.7 How to find an agency or intermediary

- Search the internet, using words as 'voluntourism', 'international volunteer work', 'volunteer program', 'volunteer project' and the equivalents in your language.

- When a magazine runs a piece on volunteer work, they will usually mention the names of local agencies in their article, so this can be a great source of information as well.

- Visit forums dedicated to people doing international volunteer work and ask for recommendations.

- Visit study abroad fairs, work experience fairs or work abroad fairs, or tourism fairs. You'll be most likely to find what you are looking for in those events that are focused on sustainable tourism, alternative vacations, meaningful travel or even specific voluntourism or volunteer vacations.

## 2.1.8 List of Agencies

This is by no means an exhaustive list of options. There exist many more very reputable agencies. Use this list as a way to start your orientation process. If you know of organizations that you would like to see added to the list, please submit them to me so they can be included in a future edition.

### INTERNATIONAL (with many national representations)

- **Ecovolunteer Program**: Two- to 13-week programs to work with animals and environmental conservation worldwide. http://www.ecovolunteer.org/
- **Projects Abroad:** (English, French, Dutch, Japanese, Hebrew, Swedish, German, Italian, Danish, Korean, Polish, Norwegian)
http://www.projects-abroad.org/

### AUSTRALIA

- **Involvement Volunteers:**  http://www.volunteering.org.au/
- **Youth Challenge Australia**: Five- to 10-week programs worldwide working with education, healthcare, environment, and more.
http://www.youthchallenge.org.au/

## CANADA

- **Canada World Youth**: Six-month program with placements worldwide on a variety of projects. http://canadaworldyouth.cwy-jcm.com/
- **Developing World Connections**: One- to six-week programs worldwide to work with community development and construction. http://www.developingworldconnections.org
- **Voluntraveler**: Children, community development, education, and healthcare projects in Peru. http://www.voluntraveler.com/

## DENMARK

- **Adventure Heart:** (Danish and English) http://www.adventureheart.com/en/forside
- **Alott:** (Danish) http://www.workandtravel.dk/

## GERMANY

- **Proyecto Mosaico:** Offers short-term volunteering opportunities in Guatemala, El Salvador, Nicaragua and Costa Rica www.promosaico.org
- **Step In** (German) http://www.stepin.de/
- **StudentsGoAbroad.com:** (German, English, Spanish, Dutch) Volunteer programs in Ecuador and Venezuela http://www.studentsgoabroad.com/
- **TravelWorks:** (German, English, French, ) http://www.travelworks.de

## THE NETHERLANDS

- **Activity International**: (Dutch) http://www.activityinternational.nl/
- **Travel Active**: (Dutch) http://www.travelactive.nl/

## NEW ZEALAND

- **Global Volunteer Network**: Two-week to five-month programs worldwide to assist with a variety of projects http://www.globalvolunteernetwork.org/
- **International Volunteer HQ**: One-week to six-month programs worldwide working with a variety of projects http://www.volunteerhq.org/

## SWITZERLAND
- **Workcamp Switzerland**: Two-week to one-year programs worldwide working with children, environment, education, and more. http://www.workcamp.ch

## UNITED KINGDOM
- **BUNAC**: Volunteer projects. Peru and Costa Rica. http://www.bunac.org
- **Concordia International Volunteers**: Two-week to one-year programs working worldwide on a variety of projects. http://www.concordiavolunteers.org.uk/
- **Globalteer**: One-week to three-month program in Asia and South America with a variety of projects. http://www.globalteer.org/
- **Global Volunteers International** (also represented in the Netherlands, Sweden, Australia, Ireland, South Africa and the US). http://www.gvi.co.uk
- **i-to-i**: One-week to three-month programs worldwide working with children, education, community development, etc. http://www.i-to-i.com
- **Real Gap Experience**: Short- and Long-term volunteer positions and internships in many different countries. http://www.realgap.com/
- **WAVA**: Two-week to one-year programs worldwide in community and conservation projects. http://www.workandvolunteer.com/

## UNITED STATES OF AMERICA
- **A Broader View**: One-week or longer programs throughout Africa, Asia, North America, and South America to work on a variety of projects. http://www.abroaderview.org/
- **AmeriSpan**: Short- and Long-term volunteer positions and internships in many different countries. http://www.amerispan.com
- **Amigos de las Americas**: Five-week to two-month youth programs in North and South America. http://www.amigoslink.org/
- **BridgeVolunteers**: Short- and Long-term volunteer positions and internships in many different countries. http://www.bridgevolunteers.org/
- **Catholic Medical Mission Board**: Three-month to one-year healthcare programs worldwide. http://www.cmmb.org/

- **Catholic Network of Volunteer Service**: One-week to three-year programs worldwide with a variety of projects.
https://www.catholicvolunteernetwork.org/
- **CC USA**: 1-week to 6-month volunteer programs in Costa Rica, Ecuador, Honduras, Panama and Peru. http://www.ccusa.com
- **CHOICE Humanitarian**: One-week programs worldwide to assist with community development and construction. http://choicehumanitarian.org/
- **Concern America**: Two-year or longer program working worldwide on a variety of projects. http://www.concernamerica.org/
- **Cross-Cultural Solutions**: Volunteer projects in Brazil, Guatemala, Costa Rica and Peru. http://www.crossculturalsolutions.org
- **Foundation for Sustainable Development**: One-month to one-year program working worldwide with business development.
http://www.fsdinternational.org/
- **Friends of the Orphans**: One-year or longer program in North and South America working with orphanages. http://www.friendsoftheorphans.org/
- **Global Citizens Network**: One- to three-week programs worldwide working on a variety of projects. http://www.globalcitizens.org/
- **Global Volunteers**: Projects in Mexico, Costa Rica, Ecuador and Peru. http://www.globalvolunteers.org
- **Globe Aware**: One-week programs worldwide with several types of work. http://www.globeaware.org/
- **Geovisions**: Short- and Long-term volunteer positions and internships in many different countries. http://www.geovisions.org
- **GVI**: One-week to one-year programs worldwide to assist with a variety of projects. http://www.gviusa.com/
- **International Student Volunteers**: Two-week programs worldwide working with community development, education, environmental conservation, and more. http://www.isvonline.com/
- **Travellers Worldwide**: Two-week to one-year programs worldwide working with education, care, sports, work experience internships, and more.
http://www.travellersworldwide.com/
- **United Planet**: One-week to one-year programs worldwide working with women's empowerment, community development, and more.
http://www.unitedplanet.org/

- **WorldTeach**: Short- and long-term programs worldwide working with children, community development, and education.
http://www.worldteach.org

### OTHER COUNTRIES
- **Travel to Teach**: Two-week education programs in Mexico, Costa Rica, Peru, el Salvador and Ecuador. http://www.travel-to-teach.org/
- **Volunteering Solutions**: Programs in Peru, Honduras, Ecuador, Costa Rica and Bolivia. (English, German, Danish, Swedish, Spanish, French, Italian, Japanese, Russian, Chinese, Korean). http://www.volunteeringsolutions.com

## 2.1.9 Tips on applying

When working with an agency, the contact between you and the organization that will receive you is limited to their application procedure. Many, but not all agencies have either a personal or a phone interview with all candidates. If your agency does not have this rule, make sure you do speak with your contact person in person or by phone anyway, as he/she can give you an idea of what is important information to include in your application, you can ask questions about how realistic your expectations are and in general get to know each other so they can make a better match with a volunteer project.

When filling out an application, you will have to provide personal information, such as address details, age, and profession. Often you'll be asked to submit your resume as well in order to have a quick overview of you professional skills. Then you'll be asked to state where you want to volunteer, when you want to start and what work you'd like to do.

 Virtually all agencies will ask you to write a motivation letter, which is the appropriate medium for communicating your goals, expectations and show your enthusiasm for being a part of a project. Use this opportunity to the fullest as your motivation letter will greatly help your agency to place you at a project that meets your needs and wishes.

Before starting to write the motivation letter, keep your list of goals and skills nearby, and make sure you state these clearly on the application. The motivation letter is all about stating clearly and honestly what you are looking for, without being inflexible. We recommend that you focus on the experience you want to have, and not on a particular project. In your motivation letter, speak about your expectations, the type of work you want to do and why, and the things you want to learn, rather than stating that you only want to work at X project, as it will be hard for the agency to determine if your preference for that project is based on real information and realistic expectations or if you have drawn your conclusion based on incorrect or incomplete information. In that case, they still won't know what you really want!

If you haven't stated this in any other part of the application, the motivation letter is also the place to explain in what kind of environment you would feel most comfortable. If you are applying to work in Costa Rica with the idea to be in the cloud forest, you don't necessarily want to be placed in a marine project on the Atlantic coast.

 You should ask the agency if your motivation letter will be forwarded to the receiving organization, as in that case you may want to adjust the letter. You can always add a short letter (preferably in Spanish, or Portuguese for Brazil) that can be sent to the organization where you'll be placed.

## 2.2 Intermediaries in the host country

In this chapter we will explain in more detail what an in-country intermediary is, how they work and what they can do for you. Similar to the last chapter, we'll give you tips on how to evaluate intermediaries and we have included a list of trusted intermediaries in various countries.

### 2.2.1 What is an in-country intermediary?

As explained in paragraph 1.1.2, volunteer agencies use the services of persons or organizations that are located in the country where the volunteer work takes place. Many of these organizations also accept direct applications and will be happy to organize your volunteer experience for you.

### 2.2.2 How do in-country intermediaries work?

An in-country agency provides you with most of the services any agency provides as well with the most obvious exception being that they are not located in your own country. This means that they may not speak your language (if that language isn't English), not have a local phone number, and that you won't be able to visit their office or an information fair.

Other differences with agencies are that in-country agencies may not be able to assist you with some of the bureaucratic aspects of your experience, such as taking out travel and/or medical insurance and purchasing your plane ticket. Finally, an important role for the agency is the cultural translation from what is the style of doing business in your destination country to how things are done in your own country. If you choose to work with an in-country intermediary you have to accept that your cultural adaptation will start from the moment you contact them! As explained in paragraph 1.1.2, the in-country contact is extremely important in the process of organizing volunteer programs, as they (should) intimately know all the organizations that receive volunteers.

The in-country agency matches volunteers with projects.

They also take care of airport pickups, arrange language classes, arrange accommodation (if necessary), and double-check with the receiving organization if they haven't forgotten about the arriving volunteer.

Once in-country, you will receive support through the in-country agency, so in that sense there is no great difference between booking through an agency or through an in-country intermediary. However, in case of any differences of opinion or problems, it can be nice to be able to contact an agent in your own country and culture to assist you.

## 2.2.3 What can you expect from an in-country agency/intermediary?

- Search the internet, using words as 'voluntourism', 'international volunteer work', 'volunteer program', 'volunteer project' and the equivalents in your language.

- You can expect that an in-country agency has a wide variety of contacts with different organizations that receive volunteers, and that they know each project personally and intimately.

- You can expect that an in-country agency can inform you of the advantages and disadvantages of each project and each geographical area where they offer programs.

- You can expect that an in-country agency can help you choose the best project for you.

- You can expect that your contact person speaks and writes reasonable English (sometimes they speak German or other languages as well).

- You can expect your agency to arrange your airport pickup, accommodation from your arrival date (you may need 1 night accommodation close to the airport before traveling to your final destination), language classes if necessary, an introduction to the organization and continued support (as needed) while working on the project.

- You can expect that an agency can bring you into contact with others who will be volunteering there at the same time.

The biggest difference between going through an agency in your country and one in your destination country is the cultural difference. While you can expect that an agency prepares you for the cultural differences, it will still communicate with you in the style you are used to. Not so with in-country intermediaries!

As explained in paragraph 1.1.3, the in-country contact is usually an organization or person with reasonable English speaking skills and with a lot of experience interacting with foreigners. However, you should expect the person to communicate with your in a high-context style, have a different attitude toward time (and deadlines, such as promises to send you information by a certain date) and will be less focused on planning details much in advance. This is what we meant in the previous paragraph- your cultural experience will already start long before you travel! If you think that vague answers, late and incomplete information, and lots of 'don't worry, we'll take care of it when you get here' will make you very nervous, you may want to consider working with an agency in your own country. If you think it will be a good way to start learning about your new culture – go right ahead! After all, your in-country intermediary will really take care of everything and everything will be alright when you get there.

## 2.2.4 Advantages/ Disadvantages

**Advantages**: Lots of service at a reasonable cost

1. One point of contact for all questions related to the volunteer project, accommodation, language classes, and practical arrangements;

2. The agencies' staff is experienced in matching candidates with projects, and is usually very good at advising you on your options;

3. Up-to-date information on the local situation on health and safety precautions, costs of living, etc.;
4. If reputable, the organization will have carefully selected the projects for a reasonable price and knows all projects personally;

5. If problems or miscommunications arise at the project, the agency can help you resolve the issues or if necessary, find a new volunteer project for you;

6. Having a person who speaks English and is (somewhat) familiar with your culture receives you when you arrive in-country and serves as a support during the experience.

**Disadvantages**: The main disadvantage is dealing with the cultural differences which can create stress when planning your trip

1. Cultural differences can complicate communication (language issues, different interpretation of time, deadlines, amount of information and preciseness of information);

2. You usually will have to communicate in (not always fluent) English or Spanish/Portuguese;

3. You usually can't choose the precise organization you are going to work for – this will be decided for you based on the information you provided on your application;

4. No help with bureaucracy such as passport- and visa applications, insurance and flights;

5. Costs; you pay a fee for the services of the intermediary.

## 2.2.5 Costs/ Cost structure

Exactly the same as with agencies in your own country, you will pay for your Accommodation, Meals (if included) and Transportation (if included).

Furthermore you'll pay for the services of the in-country contact, usually a flat fee which includes arranging a project for you, and supporting you while doing your volunteer project. Often the fee also includes an amount that will be used for donations to the various projects an organization works with.

## 2.2.6 Evaluating in-country agencies/intermediaries

If you've read the previous chapter on agencies and you've decided that you do not need the level of service that they offer, but you would like some help and security, using an in-country agency might just be exactly what you need.

You'll first need to decide with which aspects you'll need help, and then once you've decided in which 1 or 2 countries you'd like to volunteer, you need to find agencies in those countries. You might not have too many options, which makes making the choice easier!

Visit the website of the agencies and contact them by phone or by email to confirm the services they provide, the fees they charge, and – in case this is important to you – how good their English (or your language) is and how familiar they are with working with people from your cultural background.

Ask questions! All intermediaries are different. Some are specialized in a certain geographical area, others in a type of program, some have clearly defined programs and others are more flexible. Thoroughly research what you need and don't be afraid to contact several intermediaries, stating your plans and asking them how they can help you.

Confirm exactly which services the intermediary will provide for you and how much they cost. You don't want to be surprised with extra charges at a late stage.

 Verify if the organization of your choice is a member of professional associations providing you with guarantees.

## 2.2.7 How to find an in-country agency/intermediary

Search the internet, using words as 'voluntourism', 'international volunteer work', 'volunteer program', 'volunteer project' with the country name or the equivalents in Spanish (or Portuguese if you want to go to Brazil). Often, language schools have a department that arranges volunteer work, so 'language school' or 'learning Spanish' plus the name of your chosen destination could be a good starting point as well.

Visit forums dedicated to people doing international volunteer work and ask for recommendations for in-country intermediaries.

## 2.2.8 List of in-country Agencies/Intermediaries

This is by no means an exhaustive list of options. There are many more very reputable intermediaries. Use this list as a way to start your orientation process. If you know of organizations that you would like to see added to the list, please submit them to me so they can be included in a future edition.

## ARGENTINA

- **COINED:** volunteer programs and internships in various areas in Argentina, Chile, Costa Rica, Guatemala. http://www.intercoined.com/
- **Life Argentina**: Ongoing program in Argentina working with children, education, and special projects. http://www.lifeargentina.org/
- **Patagonia Volunteer**: One-month or longer program in Argentina and Chile working with administration, education, community development, and environment. http://www.patagoniavolunteer.org/

## BRAZIL

- **Fast Forward**: projects in Maceio and Sao Paulo, Brazil.
http://www.fastforward.com.br
- **Iko Poran Association**: Three-week to six-month program in and around Rio de Janeiro, Brazil with a variety of projects. http://www.ikoporan.org/
- **Institute for International Cooperation & Development**: Nine-month program working in the Bahia State, Brazil with community development, construction, education, and other projects. http://www.iicd-volunteer.org

## BOLIVIA

- **Academia Latinoamericana de Espanol**: Volunteer opportunities in various areas in Ecuador, Peru and Bolivia. http://www.latinoschool.com
- **Sustainable Bolivia**: Two-week to one-year program working with one of 26 projects in and around Cochabamba, Bolivia.
http://www.sustainablebolivia.org/

## CHILE

- **COINED**: volunteer programs and internships in various areas in Argentina, Chile, Costa Rica, Guatemala. http://www.intercoined.com/
- **National Volunteer Center Chile**: 10-week to one-year community development and education program. http://www.centrodevoluntarios.cl/
- **Patagonia Volunteer**: One-month or longer program in Argentina and Chile working with administration, education, community development, and environment. http://www.patagoniavolunteer.org/

## COLOMBIA
- **Let's Go Volunteer**: One-week to nine-month programs in Colombia working with children, teenagers, women, the elderly or in environmental conservation. http://www.letsgovolunteer.info/

## COSTA RICA
- **COINED**: volunteer programs and internships in various areas in Argentina, Chile, Costa Rica, Guatemala. http://www.intercoined.com/
- **Maximo Nivel**: One-week to two-month program in Peru, Costa Rica and Guatemala working with a variety of projects. http://www.maximonivel.com/

## DOMINICAN REPUBLIC
- **Fundacion Mahatma Gandhi**: One-week or longer program in the Dominican Republic working with a variety of projects.
http://fundacionmahatmagandhi.com/voluntariado.html

## ECUADOR
- **Ecuador Volunteer Foundation**: Volunteers stay a minimum of two weeks or two months on a variety of projects. http://www.ecuadorvolunteer.org/
- **Experiential Learning Ecuadorian Programs**: Two-week to six-month program in Ecuador on a variety of projects. http://www.elep.org/
- **Fundacion Brethren y Unida**: Ongoing program in Ecuador working with education, women's groups, and more. http://www.fbu.com.ec/
- **Academia Latinoamericana de Español**: Volunteer opportunities in various areas in Ecuador, Peru and Bolivia. http://www.latinoschool.com
- **Lead Adventures Ecuador & Galapagos**: Two-week to three-month programs working with animals, children, community development, and more. http://www.lead-adventures.com
- **Yanapuma Foundation**: One-week or longer program in Ecuador working with a variety of projects. http://www.yanapuma.org

## GUATEMALA
- **COINED**: volunteer programs and internships in various areas in Argentina, Chile, Costa Rica, Guatemala. http://www.intercoined.com/

- **INEPAS**: Three-month or longer program in Quetzaltenango, Guatemala working with a variety of projects. http://www.inepas.org/
- **Maximo Nivel**: One-week to two-month program in Peru, Costa Rica and Guatemala working with a variety of projects. http://www.maximonivel.com/

## MEXICO

- **Tlaloc**: Volunteer program in Cuernavaca, Mexico working with a variety of projects. http://www.tlaloc.com.mx/

## PERU

- **Awaiting Angels**: One-week to three-month program in Peru to work on a variety of projects. http://www.awaitingangels.org/
- **Carisma Peru**: Ongoing program in Peru to work with youth. http://www.carismaperu.org/
- **Expand Peru**: One-week or longer program in Peru working with a variety of projects. http://www.expandperu.org/
- **Hampy**: One-month or longer program in Peru working with community development and more. http://www.hampy.org/en
- **International Service Learning Alliance**: Two- to nine-week program working in Peru in various projects. http://www.isla-serve.org/
- **Academia Latinoamericana de Español**: Volunteer opportunities in various areas in Ecuador, Peru and Bolivia. http://www.latinoschool.com/
- **Luz de Esperanza**: Short-term programs in Chupaca, Peru working with a variety of construction and educational projects. http://www.peruluzdeesperanza.com/
- **Maximo Nivel**: One-week to two-month program in Peru, Costa Rica and Guatemala working with a variety of projects. http://www.maximonivel.com/
- **Mijn Bestemming Peru**: One-year program in Peru working with children, social work, and tourism. http://www.mijnbestemmingperu.nl/ (Dutch only)
- **Makikita Quykuway**: One-month or longer projects in social projects in various communities in Peru. http://volunteeringinperu.com
- **New Horizons Volunteer Program**: Three week or longer program in Ecuador working with children, elderly, education, environment, and more. http://www.voluntariosecuador.org

- **Nexos Voluntarios**: Two-week or longer program in Peru working with a variety of projects. http://www.nexosvoluntarios.org/
- **Otra Cosa**: One-month or longer program in Huanchaco and Trujillo, Peru working with a variety of projects. http://www.otracosa.nl/
- **Peru 109**: Short- and long-term social projects in Cusco, Chimbote and Trujillo, Peru. http://www.peru109.org/
- **Peru for You**: Ongoing program in various locations in Peru working with children's education. http://www.peruforyou.com/
- **VolunTeach Peru**: Two-week to six-month program working with children, community development, education, and social work.

http://www.volunteachperu.org/

## 2.2.9 Tips on applying

Much of the application process through an in-country intermediary will be the same as when applying through an agency. Inquire if you can apply in English or if you have to submit all documents in Spanish.

Below we repeat the information from paragraph 2.1.9 on applying through agencies:

When working with an agency, the contact between you and the organization that will receive you is limited to their application procedure. Many, but not all agencies have either a personal or a phone interview with all candidates. If your agency does not have this rule, make sure you do speak with your contact person in person or by phone anyway, as he/she can give you an idea of what is important information to include in your application, you can ask questions about how realistic your expectations are and in general get to know each other so they can make a better match with a volunteer project.

When filling out an application, you will have to provide personal information, such as address details, age, and profession. Often you'll be asked to submit your resume as well in order to have a quick overview of you professional skills. Then you'll be asked to state where you want to volunteer, when you want to start and what work you'd like to do.

Virtually all agencies will ask you to write a motivation letter, which is the appropriate medium for communicating your goals, expectations and show your enthusiasm for being a part of a project. Use this opportunity to the fullest as your motivation letter will greatly help your agency to place you at a project that meets your needs and wishes.

Before starting to write the motivation letter, keep your list of goals and skills nearby, and make sure you state these clearly on the application. The motivation letter is all about stating clearly and honestly what you are looking for, without being inflexible. We recommend that you focus on the experience you want to have, and not on a particular project. In your motivation letter, speak about your expectations, the type of work you want to do and why, and the things you want to learn, rather than stating that you only want to work at X project, as it will be hard for the agency to determine if your preference for that project is based on real information and realistic expectations or if you have drawn your conclusion based on incorrect or incomplete information. In that case, they still won't know what you really want!

If you haven't stated this in any other part of the application, the motivation letter is also the place to explain in what kind of environment you would feel most comfortable. If you are applying to work in Costa Rica with the idea to be in the cloud forest, you don't necessarily want to be placed in a marine project on the Atlantic coast.

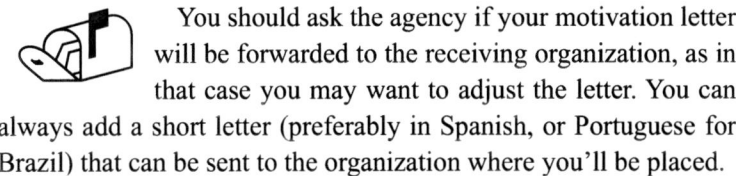
You should ask the agency if your motivation letter will be forwarded to the receiving organization, as in that case you may want to adjust the letter. You can always add a short letter (preferably in Spanish, or Portuguese for Brazil) that can be sent to the organization where you'll be placed.

## 2.3 Going direct

The two most common reasons that volunteers give for finding a volunteer project without the help of an intermediary are saving money and flexibility.

This paragraph describes how you can go about finding the best organization for your needs and wishes, and highlights those aspects that you need to take into consideration when making your decisions.

As we've explained in the previous chapters, you can volunteer at any and all organizations, based on the definition of volunteer work that this is work you don't get paid for. Below we discuss the approach to applying for volunteer positions in three segments of organizations; large international development or aid organizations, local and grassroots organizations and 'regular' organizations and businesses.

## 2.3.1 NGO's and large international organizations

Many of the large, internationally active development and aid organizations generally rely heavily on Westerners to execute projects in developing nations. Most of these employees are contracted on short contracts (6 months to 3 years) for specific projects. However, several organizations also provide opportunities for shorter volunteer commitments.

### 2.3.1.1 What can you expect when going directly to an organization

Large international organizations tend to have well-organized websites in English and often other Western languages, with lots of information about the organization and their fields of activity. Virtually all websites that we have visited have clear and comprehensive information about their volunteer opportunities, generally also detailing their application process and the costs involved. You can expect to communicate with these organizations in English and in several other Western languages.

Many of these organizations have paid aid workers on contract as well. If you're looking to make a career out of volunteering, this could be a good point to start. Naturally, you'll have to be very well qualified and be able to commit for a long time to the organization.

### 2.3.1.2 Advantages/ Disadvantages

These large organizations often have a Western based organizational culture, which can help you if you are concerned about adapting to the Latin American way of working. You will always be immersed in the Latin

American culture when you are working there, but it can be very comforting if the arrangements and pre-departure contacts are conducted in a more Western spirit!

As is the nature of large organizations, they need to be structured and organized to be able to function. The advantage is that you will be able to find out quickly if there are volunteer positions available in the area where you want to work, if you're qualified for the work, what the costs are and which application process you should follow. The disadvantage is that there will be little to no flexibility regarding your personal preferences or situation. It will be a case of 'take it or leave it'.

### 2.3.1.3 Costs/ Cost structure

The cost structure is similar to that of agencies, as these organizations have offices, often in Western countries, and staff dedicated to offering, preparing and organizing volunteer experiences. Volunteering opportunities (not the paid positions) can be fairly costly, but do include the type of services you expect from an agency; organization and confirmation of the volunteer project before you travel; accommodation and meals; services on-site from an English speaking volunteer coordinator; in-country transportation if needed.

When highly qualified and signing up for long deployments (usually at least 6 or 12 months) you may be receiving a stipend for living expenses and transportation. These assignments lie outside of the scope of this book.

For short term volunteer projects you should not expect any compensation.

## 2.3.1.4 Evaluating organizations

It is fairly easy to determine if the organization can give you the experience you're looking for, as they have easily accessible and comprehensive information about volunteering, through their websites and local offices.

Refer back to your list of goals for your experience and compare that to what the organization can offer you. Do not expect that these organizations are flexible or able to adapt a program to your needs or wishes. You can expect the organization and your contact to be serious, reliable, organized and well-aware of the challenges of working in Latin America.

## 2.3.2 Local/Grassroots organizations

In this section we discuss applying to local Latin American organizations. These are the organizations most people immediately think of when considering doing volunteer work. Local or national initiatives run by a few professionals, heavily understaffed and underfunded, and in dire need of help!

## 2.3.2.1 What can you expect when going directly to an organization

You can expect a full immersion in Latin American culture from the first time you contact the organization. Don't expect people to speak much English, your email may not arrive and if it arrives you probably won't receive an answer. Organizations will react open, friendly and enthusiastic to your proposal (unless they've had negative experiences with volunteers cutting their commitments short or otherwise not fitting in the organization) but will have difficulty committing to receiving you if you apply far in advance. Communication throughout the process will be spotty, with internet connections and phone lines down frequently. You'll hear many 'don't worry's' and you'll have to try to take that advice to heart. You will not get much written or precise information. They may or may not help you arrange accommodation.

Upon arrival, someone, probably the person you've been communicating with, will likely be there to receive you (or will arrive shortly if held up somewhere). He/she will introduce you to your colleagues and make you feel welcome. Probably someone will accompany you to your accommodation if this is possible, whether they helped you arrange it or not.

Depending on whether they have received many other volunteers in the past, you meet colleagues who treat you as a guest and don't want to you work (see paragraph 1.6). If the organization has a lot of experience receiving volunteers, present or past volunteers may have prepared documentation or an introduction for you to make you familiar with your tasks.

If you act with cultural sensitivity and commit to more than a few weeks – building up rapport with your coworkers and manager - you will have a lot of freedom and flexibility to make suggestions, start activities or initiatives of your own, and/or be involved with the organization on a deeper level.

## 2.3.2.2 Advantages/ Disadvantages

**Advantages**: You choose the specific project you want to work for yourself and the costs are low to reasonable

1. You get a much better feel for the people and the atmosphere in the organization before you make your final decision;

2. You decide yourself which organization you would like to work for;

3. You can have a total immersion experience, dealing only with Latin Americans and the Latin American way of working;

4. You can end up at very interesting, unique projects that rarely receive volunteers;

5. This is the most flexible way of organizing a volunteer experience;

6. Up-to-date information on the local situation on health and safety precautions, costs of living, etc.;

7. You pay no overhead to other organizations; when reputable, any money you pay goes directly to the organization.

**Disadvantages**: Cultural differences and no 'third-party' support

1. Cultural differences can complicate communication (language issues, different

interpretation of time, deadlines, amount of information and preciseness of information);

2. You usually will have to communicate in (not always fluent) English or Spanish/Portuguese;

3. Emails may not arrive or do not get answered. Assisting volunteers is not the core tasks of the organization – which is usually understaffed as it is;

4. No help with bureaucracy such as passport- and visa applications and insurance;

5. Usually no help with arranging flights, in-country transportation and accommodation.

6. Little to no onsite introduction or support. You really have to fend for yourself.

## 2.3.2.3 Costs/ Cost structure

As there is little overhead related to proving services for you, you should not have to pay large fees. At the same time, many organizations charge an application fee, for two reasons; first, to discourage frivolous applications, and second, to compensate the time that a staff member spends answering your questions, receiving you and introducing you to the organization and your tasks.

As for the frivolous applications; those organizations who receive many volunteers will have noticed that sometimes they get contacted by prospective volunteers who ask an enormous amount of detailed questions (to the level of; how much does a bottle of shampoo cost?)

but never end up applying, or volunteers who ask the organization to commit to receiving them months in advance, but never show up or leave again after a few days. These organizations may establish a reasonable application fee (say US$100) to pre-select the more serious candidates. You should avoid paying a recurring (weekly or monthly) fee or if you do, the fees should get significantly lower for longer commitments.

Some larger organizations have accommodation or arrange accommodation for their volunteers. Again, you can expect that the organization does not make a profit on the accommodation. To check if you're being quoted a reasonable price, check with local hotels or hostels, or check the accommodation price that you would pay if going through an international agency. Alternatively, you can commit to a short period in this accommodation and compare onsite if you're paying a reasonable price.

You may or may not receive meals at your volunteer project and you may or may not have to contribute to the cost of these. Verify in advance and adjust your budget accordingly.

## 2.3.2.4 Evaluating receiving organizations

We have mentioned before that also in the development and aid sector, there are less reputable organizations. As a volunteer, you can come into contact with such organizations, and you can become a victim of them. We assume that you genuinely want to contribute to the development and wellbeing of a community, and that you want your physical and financial contribution to be used for that community and not to enrich the owner/director of the volunteer project.

Without becoming paranoid, we recommend that you evaluate each prospective organization with a critical eye to avoid becoming a victim to a volunteering scam.

Serious organizations will require a lot from their volunteers! You can expect them to have requirements for age, skills/education, minimum commitment time, language skills, etc. You can re-read the section on the 'business' of volunteering to understand why it is logical for organizations to have requirements, and how certain factors can offset a lack of certain skills (paragraph 1.6).

The website or information of the projects contains the names of the owners/directors of the project, pictures and their contact information – if they are identifiable this means they are accountable.

The organization does not ask for (vague) cash donations but can specify exactly which materials they need. It should not be obligatory (but there is no harm in the organization recommending it) to bring donations, either in cash or in materials. It should also not be obligatory to book their in-house Spanish classes or accommodation (or if they do the price should be reasonable and it should be obvious that there are no alternatives, such as when staying in a national park).

Make sure that you ask for an example of the type and range of tasks you will be performing, and an indication of how much time you will spend on each

task. Don't expect any precise answers, and don't expect that the reality will be exactly like that, it's just not in the Latin culture to be precise (for more information on Latin American cultures, see paragraph 3.1). What you want to know is an indication of what to expect.

As mentioned before, if you'll be volunteering at a turtle rescue project it's unrealistic to expect that you'll be observing turtles and cuddling baby turtles all the time, and more realistic to prepare for exhausting all-nighters plowing up and down the beach to make sure poachers don't get a chance to rob the eggs and seeing only few turtles up close.

Some organizations will be brutally honest with you, even exaggerating, just to make sure you won't quit on them after a few days. Others might be so enthusiastic about you coming that they will make the job sound more beautiful than it really is. Keep an open mind towards these possible reactions and try to obtain objective information (for example from past volunteers) regarding what to expect exactly.

## 2.3.3 'Regular' (non-aid) organizations and businesses

These organizations encompass all organizations that do not fall into the former two categories. We expect that you want to contact this type of organization if you are looking for a volunteer position or internship in an area where you can apply or develop your particular skills and experience.

## 2.3.3.1 What can you expect when going directly to an organization

These organizations are not involved in development or aid work, so they do not have (much) experience in receiving foreign volunteers or interns. You should be prepared to explain carefully who you are, what you want and what the organization can expect from you. You'd have to explain the concept of receiving a foreign volunteer or intern, and convince them that it will be a positive experience for them. Latin Americans are generally less prepared to take risks than North-Americans (amongst others) and organizations are more hierarchical. You need to make sure you're communicating with a person who has the authority to take the decision whether to accept you.

When applying to a business, it´s even more important than in non-profit organizations that your presence has a benefit for the organization. As your colleagues and manager will have to invest time and resources in you, you will be expected to adopt a serious work ethic and comply with working hours, deadlines and office policy, even though you won't receive a stipend or salary.

Do not expect any assistance with your practical arrangements (flight, visa, insurance, accommodation, etc.).

Do not expect your colleagues to speak English or have any knowledge of your culture. You will be expected to behave 'normal' – read: according to their cultural norms – from the moment you contact the organization. Preparation in cultural differences and effective intercultural communication is necessary for a positive experience.

## 2.3.3.2 Advantages/ Disadvantages

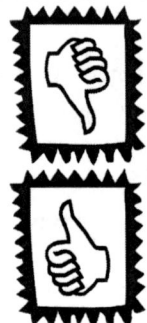

These are the same as when applying to a local social/aid organization directly (see paragraph 1.3.2.2), with the note that the pre-arrival and onsite support will likely be less as these organizations receive less volunteers/interns.

At the same time, businesses are less understaffed and you probably have a much more clearly defined project to undertake.

## 2.3.3.3 Costs/ Cost structure

Again, these are comparable to those at local/ grassroots organizations (see paragraph 1.3.2.3).

## 2.3.3.4 Evaluating 'regular' organizations and businesses

You are much less likely to run into 'volunteer scams' when applying to regular businesses. We do recommend that you always use your common sense, and don't accept offers that seem too good to be true - they usually are!

For evaluating businesses we recommend that you focus on the tasks you will perform. You've probably made the decision to contact a certain type of organization because you are looking to contribute your specific skills and work experience, or wanting to gain specific work experience. Therefore, the actual work you are going to do should be the focus of your search.

We have mentioned before that exactness is not a strong point of the Latin American cultures and it will be very difficult to get firm confirmation on anything. You'll have to strike a balance as to how much precise information/promises you need before committing to the experience, against accepting the cultural differences.

Finding a contact person you trust and who understands your situation will be crucial. We strongly recommend that you contact as many organizations as you can, and that you contact them by phone as well as email (to strengthen the connection and trust between you and the organization), so that you can get a good feel for the differences between the organizations, before you make your final choice.

If you need university credits for your internship, then it's even more important to make sure you will be able to provide your school with the documentation and results they need to approve the credits.

## 2.3.4 How to find an organization

It must sound boring by now, but the best source of information is the internet. The best approach is to search in Spanish, although more and more organizations have websites in English these days.

## 2.3.5 List of organizations

This is by no means an exhaustive list of options. There exist many more very reputable projects. Use this list as a way to start your orientation process. If you know of organizations that you would like to see added to the list, please submit them to me so they can be included in a future edition.

# A

- **ACDI/VOCA**: Two-week or longer programs worldwide for mid-career professionals to assist with business development and more.
http://www.acdivoca.org/

- **AEC-TEA Association**: Three-month to one-year project in Brazil to assist with education and community service initiatives.
http://www.aec-tea.org/

- **Ak'Tenamit**: Volunteers stay a minimum of three to six months in Guatemala to assist with all aspects of Q'eqchi community improvement project.
http://www.aktenamit.org/

- **Amanecer Cochabamba**: Six-month or longer program in Bolivia to work with homeless women and children. http://www.amanecer-bolivia.org/

- **Amazon Waterfalls Association**: Two-week or longer program to work with a conservation committee. http://www.amazonwaterfalls.org/

- **Amigos de Iracambi**: One-month or longer programs in Brazil to assist with rainforest conservation. http://www.iracambi.com/

- **Andean Bear Conservation Project**: Two-week or longer program in Ecuador to work with bears. http://www.andeanbear.org/

- **Andean Outreach Program**: One-week or longer program in Peru to work with children's education programs. http://www.andeanoutreach.org/

- **Animal Aware**: Two-week or longer program in Guatemala to rescue and rehabilitate domestic animals. http://www.animalaware.org/

- **The Ara Project**: One- to two-month program in Costa Rica to work at a macaw breeding and rehabilitation center. http://www.thearaproject.org/

- **ARCAS**: One-week or longer project in Guatemala to work with wildlife preservation and other projects. http://www.arcasguatemala.com/

- **Artesania Sorata**: Two-month or longer program in Bolivia to work with children's education, business development, and more.
http://www.artesaniasorata.com/

- **Asociacion Nuevos Horizontes**: One-month or longer program in Guatemala to work with children's education. http://www.ahnh.org/

- **ASVO**: One-month or longer program in Costa Rica to work with environmental conservation initiatives. http://www.asvocr.org/

## B

- **Bay Islands Conservation Association**: One- to three-month program in Honduras to work with environmental conservation. http://www.bicautila.org/
- **BEMELSA**: 3-months and Langer educational program in Chincha, Peru. http://www.bemelsa.org/
- **Bilingual Education for Central America**: One-year or longer program in Honduras to assist with children's education. http://www.becaschools.org/
- **Bruce Peru**: One-month or longer programs in Peru to work on a variety of projects. http://www.bruceperu.org/

## C

- **Caribbean Conservation Corporation**: One- to three-week program in Costa Rica to work with sea turtles and other projects. http://www.conserveturtles.org/
- **Casa do Caminho**: Six-month to two-year program in Brazil to work with children and families. http://www.casadocaminhobrasil.org/
- **Casa Guatemala**: Education project in orphanage Casa Guatemala in Rio Dulce, Guatemala. http://www.casa-guatemala.org/
- **Casa Hogar los Gorriones**: One-month or longer program in Peru to work with children. http://www.casahogarlosgorriones.org/
- **Casas de la Esperanza**: Ongoing community development and construction projects in Nicaragua. http://www.casas-de-la-esperanza.org/
- **Ceiba Foundation for Tropical Conservation**: One-week to three-month programs in Ecuador on a variety of projects. http://www.ceiba.org/
- **Centro Educativo Nanta**: Six-month to one-year projects in Bolivia to work with indigenous children. http://www.centro-nanta.org/
- **Charles Darwin Foundation**: 2-3 month or longer programs in Ecuador to work with environmental conservation. http://www.darwinfoundation.org/
- **Cloud Forest School**: Three-week or longer program in Costa Rica to assist with a school. http://cloudforestschool.org/
- **Cofradia's Bilingual School**: Three-week or longer program in Honduras to work in a school. http://www.cofradiaschool.com/
- **Colibris Women's Artisan Cooperative**: Two-week or longer project in Ecuador working with women's groups. http://www.colibrisecuador.org/

- **Common Hope**: Community developments programs in Guatemala http://www.commonhope.org/
- **Comuna de Rhiannon**: Two-week or longer program in Ecuador working with organic farming and construction. http://www.rhiannon-community.org/
- **Comunidad Inti Wara Yassi**: 15-day or longer program in Bolivia working with animals and environmental conservation. http://www.intiwarayassi.org/
- **Comunidad Nueva Alianza**: Two-day or longer program working in Guatemala on an organic farm. http://www.comunidadnuevaalianza.org/
- **Condortrekkers**: One-week or longer program in Bolivia, where volunteers lead tours and assist with other projects. http://condortrekkers.org/
- **Creative Corners**: One-month or longer program working in North and South America for children's education. http://www.creative-corners.com/
- **Creciendo Juntos Foundation**: One-week or longer program providing administrative duties in a medical/dental care clinic in Bolivia. http://www.freewebs.com/creciendo-juntos/
- **Crees Expeditions**: Two-week or longer program in Peru working with community development and environmental conservation. http://www.crees-expeditions.com/

## E

- **El Centro de la Niña Trabajadora**: Two-month or longer program in Ecuador to work with young women. http://www.cenitecuador.org/
- **El Nahual Language Center**: One-week or longer programs in Guatemala to work with education. http://www.languageselnahual.com/
- **El Porvenir**: One- to two-week environmental conservation program in Nicaragua. http://elporvenir.org/

## F

- **Fabretto Children's Foundation**: Long-term program in Nicaragua on children, health, and community development projects. http://www.fabretto.org/
- **FairMail**: Two-month or longer program in Asia and South America on arts, children, education, and social work projects. http://www.fairmail.info/
- **Fauna Paraguay**: Ongoing program in Paraguay working with animals and environmental conservation. http://www.faunaparaguay.com/

## 2 • Finding a Volunteer position

- **Fundacion Arte del Mundo**: One-month or longer program in Ecuador working with art and English education, as well as library assistance. http://www.artedelmundoecuador.com/
- **Fundacion CHOL-CHOL**: Three-month or longer program in Chile working with business development. http://www.cholchol.org/
- **Fundacion Delpia**: Three-week or longer program in Bolivia working with indigenous community development. http://www.fundacion-delpia.org/
- **Fundacion Luz del Mundo**: Teaching English at local children's home in Santa Cruz, Bolivia. http://www.volunteersouthamerica.net/LuzDelMundo/ldm_index.htm
- **Fundacion de Proteccion Animal**: Three-month or longer program in Ecuador working with animals, business development, and more. http://www.fpa-ecuador.org/
- **Fundacion Salvacion**: Children's home in Huehuetenango, Guatemala. http://en.fundacionsalvacion.net
- **Fundacion Zoobreviven**: Two-week or longer program in Ecuador working with environmental conservation. http://www.zoobreviven.org/
- **Fundecoipa**: Two-week or longer program in Ecuador working with a variety of projects. http://www.fundecoipa.com/

## G

- **Galapagos ICE**: One-week or longer program in Ecuador to assist with education, environment, and healthcare. http://galapagosice.org/
- **Grupo Ecologico de la Costa Verde**: Two-month or longer programs in Mexico working with sea turtles and conservation. http://www.project-tortuga.org/

## H

- **Habitat for Humanity**: One-week or longer construction programs worldwide. http://www.habitat.org/
- **Hacienda Tranquila**: One- to 12-week program in Galapagos working with community, environment, and social issues. http://www.haciendatranquila.com/
- **Helping Honduras Kids**: One-week or longer children's education program. http://www.helpinghonduraskids.org/

- **Hogar de Esperanza**: Peruvian Christian-based orphanage accepting volunteers for short- and long stays in a variety of roles. http://perukids.com
- **Hogar Miguel Magone**: Two-week or longer programs in Guatemala to work with children's education initiatives http://www.hogarmiguelmagone.com/
- **Honduras Children**: Eight-week or longer programs in El Porvenir, Honduras working with childcare, education, and more http://www.honduraschildren.org/
- **Horizon School Peru**: Short-term programs in Trujillo, Peru giving free English classes to children and adults. http://www.horizonperu.com/

## I

- **Incawasi**: 2 months or longer program in Cajamarca, Peru working with children's education initiatives. http://www.incawasi.org.pe/
- **International Senior Lawyers Project**: One-month to several-year program worldwide working to provide legal services and guidance. http://www.islp.org/
- **International Smile Power Foundation**: Short-term program working in Bolivia and Guatemala on dental care initiatives. http://www.smilepower.org/

## J

- **Jatun Sacha**: Two-week or longer program in national reserves in Ecuador working with research, education, reforestation, and more.
http://www.jatunsacha.org/

## K

- **Kids World Wide**: 1-month and longer commitment in children's homes in various countries. http://www.kidsworldwide.org/

## L

- **La Casa Hogar Los Gorriones**: Orphanage in Ayacucho, Peru, where volunteers can help caring for the children, work in the restaurant or in the office. http://www.casahogarlosgorriones.org/
- **La Esperanza Granada**: Six-week or longer program in Granada, Nicaragua working with children's education and community development projects. http://www.la-esperanza-granada.org/
- **La Tortuga Feliz**: One-week or longer sea turtle monitoring program in Costa Rica. http://www.latortugafeliz.com

- **Las Mercedes Reforestation Project**: Two-week or longer program in Nicaragua working with reforestation, environmental conservation, and more. http://nicaraguareforestationproject.org/
- **Long Way Home**: Short-term program in Comolapa, Guatemala working with a variety of construction, environmental and social projects. http://www.longwayhomeinc.org/

## M

- **Maya Pedal**: Volunteer opportunities in cycling related positions in San Andres Itzapa, Guatemala. http://www.mayapedal.org/
- **Merazonia**: Two-week or longer program in Mera, Ecuador working with animals, construction, gardening, and trail building. http://www.merazonia.org/
- **Mosoq Ayllu**: Short-term program in Cusco, Peru working with children, education, healthcare, and more. http://www.volunteering-peru.com

## N

- **New Era Galapagos Foundation**: One-month or longer community development and education program in Ecuador.
http://neweragalapagos.blogspot.com
- **Ninos de Guatemala**: 5-weeks and longer educational opportunities in Ciudad Vieja and Antigua, Guatemala. http://www.ninosdeguatemala.org/
- **Nuestros Pequenos Hermanos**: International 1-year commitments in orphanages in many Latin American and Caribbean countries. 2-3 month commitments in Haiti and the Dominican Republic. http://www.nph.org/

## P

- **Peace Villages Foundation**: Ongoing program in Santa Elena, Venezuela working with children, education, healthcare, research, and more.
http://www.peacevillages.org/
- **Pina Palmera**: Six-month or longer program in Mexico working with community development, healthcare, special needs, and more.
http://www.pinapalmera.org/
- **Pinocho School**: Teaching English at a local school in Quijarro, in the Bolivian Amazon. http://www.volunteersouthamerica.net/Pinocho/pin_index.htm

- **Pisco Sin Fronteras**: Two-week and longer construction and community development program in Pisco, Peru. http://www.piscosinfronteras.org/
- **Platanitos Turtle Camp**: Ongoing sea turtle protection program in Puerto Vallarta, Mexico. http://www.seaturtlecamp.org/
- **PRETOMA**: One-week to five-month sea turtle protection project in Costa Rica. http://www.pretoma.org/
- **Primeros Pasos**: One-month or longer healthcare program in Palajunoj, Guatemala. http://www.primerospasos.org
- **Pronino Honduras**: Six-month or longer program working with career training, children, and more. http://www.pronino.org/
- **Proyecto Montezuma**: One-week to two-month rural education program in Montezuma, Costa Rica. http://www.proyectomontezuma.org/

## Q

- **Quetzaltrekkers**: Three-month or longer program working in Guatemala and Nicaragua as a hiking guide. http://www.quetzaltrekkers.com/

## R

- **Radiant Futures**: Orphanage in Chiapas, Mexico.
http://www.radiantfutures.org/
- **Rainforest Biodiversity Group**: One-month or longer program in Costa Rica working with environmental education and similar activities.
http://www.rainforestbiodiversity.org/
- **RCDP International Volunteer**: One-week to three-month programs in Costa Rica, Guatemala, Ecuador and Peru working on a variety of projects http://www.rcdpinternationalvolunteer.org/
- **Reserva Ecologica de Guapiacu**: Two-month or longer program in Brazil working with environment, education, reforestation, and more.
http://www.regua.co.uk/

## S

- **Safe Passage / Camino Seguro**: 5-weeks to 1 year positions in education in Guatemala City, Guatemala. http://www.safepassage.org/
- **Santa Lucia Ecuador Cloud Forest Reserve**: Organic farming project in Ecuador. http://www.santaluciaecuador.com/

- **Seeds of Hope**: One-month or longer program in Peru working with children's education projects. http://www.peruseeds.org/

- **Seeds of Learning**: One- to two-week construction projects in El Salvador and Nicaragua. http://www.seedsoflearning.org/

- **Sharing Dreams-Peru**: Two-week to three-month program in Peru working with community improvement and educational projects.
http://volunteering-inperu.blogspot.com

- **Shiripuno**: One-month to one-year program in Amazonial Ecuador working with research, environment, construction, and more.
http://www.shiripunoresearch.org/

- **Spanish School in Bariloche**: Two-week or longer program in Argentina working with community development, education, and more.
http://www.spanishinbariloche.com/

- **Spanish School La Montana**: One-month or longer program in Argentina working with environment, social work, and more. http://www.lamontana.com/

- **Sumak Kawsay Yachay**: Community and Educational volunteer opportunities in Salasaca, Ecuador. http://www.skyecuador.org/

- **Supporting Kids in Peru**: One-month or longer community improvement program in Trujillo, Peru. http://www.skipperu.org/

- **Students Helping Honduras**: One-week construction project in Honduras
http://www.studentshelpinghonduras.org/

## T

- **Tandana Foundation**: One- to five-week program in Ecuador working with community development, education, healthcare, and reforestation.
http://www.tandanafoundation.org/

- **Teach English, Volunteer**: 4-month and longer programs teaching English in Ecuadorian elementary schools. http://www.teach-english-volunteer.com/

- **Teach Huaraz Peru**: One-month or longer program working with education in Huaraz, Peru. http://www.teachhuarazperu.org/

- **Tinkuy Peru**: One-week or longer program in Huancayo, Peru working with children. Also short-term construction possible. http://www.peruandeankids.org/

### V

- **VEGlobal**: Three-month or longer programs in Chile working with children, education, and business administration. http://www.ve-global.org/
- **Volunteer Peten**: One- to three-month program in San Andres, Guatemala working with agriculture, environment, education, and trail building. http://www.volunteerpeten.org/

### W

- **WIDECAST Latin American Programs**: One-week or longer sea turtle protection and environmental conservation programs in Costa Rica. http://www.latinamericanseaturtles.org/
- **Working Boys' Center**: One-year or longer program in Ecuador working with job training, education, and more. http://www.workingboyscenter.org/

### Y

- **You Volunteer**: Community service and educational project in the Ecuadorian Amazon. http://www.youvolunteer.org/

## 2.3.6 Tips on applying

Contacting organizations directly generally takes more time but allow you to present yourself and your plans directly to the people you'll be working with. A direct communication flow can help you to quickly develop a feel for the organization and how you would fit in there. It can help you with your choice. As mentioned in the section about intermediaries, by no means limit yourself to one organization!

You'll probably have to contact a large number of potential organizations in order to find one with whom you can come to an agreement. Especially if you are limited to a narrow time frame, it may take some time to find an organization that needs a pair of helping hands at exactly the same time, when there is no overlap with possible other volunteers.

It's more common for Latin American organizations than Western organizations to not answer email, so you might want to place a phone call to the organizations you are interested in.

# 3

## Preparing For Working In Latin America

## 3.1 Culture

It's been mentioned before, and here I say it again: Latin American cultures are very different from Anglo-Saxon cultures, and unless you are Latin, are raised in a Latino family or have lived in a Latin country before, you will experience severe culture shock! Now, don't get too nervous over this, 'severe culture shock' is not a bad thing, or something to avoid. We state it this way because we want you to be prepared for it (at least as far as you can prepare yourself for culture shock) and not feel like you are failing if there are some moments that you feel a bit lonely, lost or depressed. The sooner you realize it is all part of a natural and unavoidable process, the smoother the 'ride' will be.

### 3.1.1 Now, what is culture shock, then?

When you first arrive in a new country, you're eager and happy – everything is new and exciting, and you'll probably love your new life. This is the honeymoon phase. This phase luckily lasts quite a while, especially in Latin America where the cultures (I don't want to insinuate that all of Latin America's cultures are the same!!!) are pretty likable over all. However, after a few weeks (roughly said, this can be as little as 2 or as much as 10 weeks, roughly said), the honeymoon phase is over and reality sets in. Especially when you're not on holiday, but volunteering you are very much confronted by the every day realities of your new culture. You start seeing things that you don't like about the new culture, things that are done 'better' back home. For Anglo-Saxons, these things can be the preparation and planning we put into our jobs, being on time for

appointments, or the direct manner of communicating with each other. When you start to have these little irritations, you know you've arrived at the second phase.

The irritation phase leads straight into the big dip (as shown in the graph as the lowest point, the third stage) – this is the worst phase of culture shock. Here, little irritations have developed into flat out rejection of the new culture. You may think that although superficially it all seems pretty nice (you remember your honeymoon phase) on closer inspection this culture turns out to be horrible, machista, old fashioned, false, etc etc etc….. You're frustrated, tired, a bit depressed, maybe you feel lonely, homesick or helpless. Luckily, this phase doesn't last very long, anywhere from a few days to a few weeks at most. At this point you may turn to hanging out with people from your own or similar cultures, eating familiar foods and speaking your own language as much as possible. Don't feel bad about it - this is perfectly ok if it helps you get through the difficult days!

Once you've passed the worst period, you enter stage four, adaptation, when you slowly start to feel better and when you start to develop ways to deal with the new culture, accepting the positive aspects and learning to work with the parts you don't like as much. This is the phase where awareness and knowledge of culture shock and coping mechanisms can make all the difference.

Stage four gradually passes into stage five: you've found your balance. You're at home in your new country, you have your favorite foods, places to go out, you've made friends, you have your daily routine…. you're at home!

I haven't yet met anybody who didn't experience any culture shock, but I have seen huge variations in the level of it. We hope that

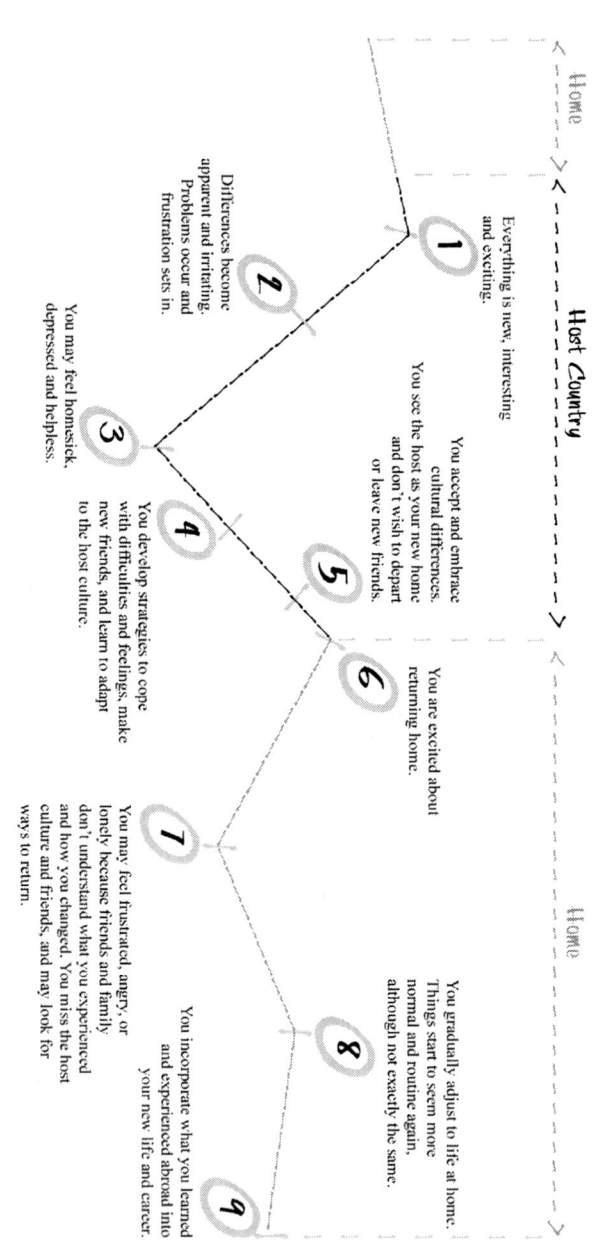

our explanation will help, so culture shock won't hit you unaware and that our tips on how to deal with it will help you experience a less steep downward curve, and to get out of the negative part sooner.

A last warning; there is such a thing as reverse culture shock, and many of you will experience it when returning home! Refer back to the figure; upon returning home you're happy to see everybody, to be back home in the familiar environment, and full of exciting stories to tell (stage 6). However, after a few days or weeks, you start missing your host countries' culture. You may also feel a bit disappointed in your friends and family as they don't understand what you've experienced, and they may appear unsupportive or uninterested. There may also be parts of your own culture that you see in a new light now you've experienced a different way of life. This is stage 7. Here you need to go through the same process as before; you feel pretty bad for a while, but you adapt again and regain a balance (stage 8 and 9) where you've incorporated your experiences in the home country in your character, norms and values and aspirations for your life and career.

## 3.1.2 What is culture?

We are aware that you, the reader of this book, can come from any culture, but at the same time we also know that most volunteers to Latin America

come from Anglo-Saxon or Germanic cultures, such as the United States, Canada, Western Europe (except France, French-speaking Switzerland and Southern European countries), Australia and New Zealand. That's why we will focus on the differences between the Anglo-Saxon culture and the Latin American culture. In doing this, we will have to make great generalizations. Not only will absolutely none of my readers come from 'the' Anglo-Saxon culture, nor will

any of you travel to 'the' Latin American culture.

And we're not even touching on the differences in personality between you, which - by the way - are much more varied than any difference between cultures. Please adapt my general advice to your own culture and personality. If you're interested in knowing more precise differences, email me and I'll send you more detailed information about the differences between the culture where you are from and the culture you are traveling to.

For my explanations about culture I use the theory of my fellow countryman Geert Hofstede, one of the top researchers on cultural differences. He developed the 'five dimensions of culture', where each dimension is represented by a scale between two extremes. Every culture that is investigated receives scores representing a position on the scale, on every one of the five dimensions.

These are the dimensions:

Individualism - Collectivism
Masculinity - Femininity
High Power distance - Low Power Distance
Uncertainty Avoidance - Uncertainty Tolerance
Long term orientation - Short term orientation

Between the Anglo-Saxon and the Latin American cultures you find the biggest differences on the scores on the Individualism-Collectivism, Power Distance and Uncertainty Avoidance scales.

## Individualism-Collectivism

The Anglo-Saxon cultures have the highest scores of all countries on the individualistic side of the 'Individualistic-Collectivistic' scale, while the Latin American cultures generally are much more collectivistic. This difference is expressed, for example, that in a collectivistic culture children are brought up to form part of a group. They think more in terms of 'we' and are taught to act and behave in ways that are good for the group. The group can be the extended family, village, tribe, or all colleagues at work. Everything they do reflects on the group, so there is a high level of social control and individual decisions (what to study, whom to marry) are made bearing in mind the needs of the group. This results in more homogeneity in behavior, people getting jobs and promotions thanks to who they know not what they know, and a higher level of conservatism, as 'experiments' (in dress, education, profession, etc) which turn out badly do not only affect the person but his/her whole in-group, and are therefore very risky.

People from individualistic countries are trained to make the best of their talents, to fulfill their dreams, to form their own opinion and make their own choices. You can see that this is a very different way of making decisions. The people from individualistic cultures should try to respect the decisions made by people from collectivistic cultures. We have a tendency to jump to (negative) conclusions if we see that a business owner employs his nephew, or that a talented musician decides to study law. Try to see these situations in the light of their different view of life and responsibilities.

## Power Distance

Research on differences in Power Distance shows that most Latin American countries know a High Power Distance, while most Anglo-Saxon cultures have a low score on Power Distance. This means that in Anglo-Saxon cultures power is earned, limited to a certain aspect of life (family, position at work, position at the sports club) and temporary (for as long as the position is held). In Latin America, power is ascribed, meaning that a person is powerful because of his/her social position, age, or position within the family (such as being the eldest son). Power pervades all aspects of life and as it's ascribed, once it's achieved, it's permanent. So, while your boss in Germany is only your boss at work, in Mexico he also is your boss in your private life, so you would take your boss' opinion seriously in matters of choosing a partner, hobby's or where to live. You will also show more respect to elders, just because they are older! Your boss may have gotten his position because he is a member of a family with high social status and power in the community.

When arriving into a high power distance culture, be careful to observe the people you get in contact with and to respect their position. You may not consider them powerful (when assessing their situation based on your own norms and values) but as everyone around you does (this includes the powerful as well as the less powerful people – an important aspect from the high power distance culture is that people without power also accept these power differences as normal), please don't disrespect them as this will unnerve everybody. If you want to discuss something with a person who has a higher power status than you, try to do this in a way where he/she will not be embarrassed, for example in a private conversation which you start with stroking their ego a bit.

## Uncertainty Avoidance

Uncertainty avoidance relates to the ability of people to deal with ambiguity and uncertainty in everyday life. Most countries actually score fairly high on this scale, except a few, notably Jamaica and the Scandinavic countries. Anglo-Saxon cultures score relatively low (with the exception of Belgium) and Latin American cultures have the highest scores of all. Now, what does this mean for you? People from uncertainty avoidance cultures feel uncomfortable in unstructured situations. Maybe it makes you laugh to think that it's especially the Latin Americans who score high on this, as these cultures are known for their lax attitude towards punctuality, planning and organizing!

> What you need to realize, is that in fact Latin Americans live in a very structured society, only it's structured in a for outsiders invisible way, such as by unwritten rules. The division of gender roles, family obligations, the way free time is used (activities, hobbies), dress codes, all these aspects are strictly regulated and don't allow for much deviation from the norm. Uncertainty avoidance cultures tend to be cultures where display of emotions and discussions are acceptable ways of communication - they serve to get to the truth, as of course there can be only 1 correct answer to any question (i.e. they cannot be any uncertainty). If you've been to a Latin American family dinner, you know what I mean!

In cultures that have low uncertainty avoidance, people accept that there can be different version of the truth, and they highly value harmony and friendship.

## 3.1.3 High vs. Low context communication

A further aspect of Latin American cultures that is different from most Anglo-Saxon cultures is the way they communicate. Latin Americans generally communicate high context, whereas Anglo-Saxons prefer low context communication.

The terms high context communication and low context communication are used to explain a difference in the use and the meaning of words. High context communication means that much remains unsaid in a conversation. A few words can convey a complicated message as many customs, ideas, and expectation are understood as being <u>implicit</u> among the conversation partners. Non-verbal communication, gestures, sighs, and silences are extremely important in conveying the message.

Low context cultures speak much more explicitly. In low context cultures you can take the words that someone speaks much more literally, and you'll find that information is often written down, formalized and accessible to you.

You can imagine how difficult it can be for you, coming from a more literal communication style, to understand what someone from a high context communication style is trying to tell you. For you to understand a high context message, you need to have a shared (cultural) framework. With this I mean that you need shared internalized understandings (background information, customs and experiences) to be able to correctly interpret the implicit message which is NOT said with words.

Low-context cultures can seem 'cold' to people from high-context cultures as these cultures tend to be more rule-oriented, relationships are functional and do not always pervade all aspects of life. We place much importance on written information and references to handbooks, contracts or other written documentation. Don't expect to find much written information in Latin America! Many volunteers complain about the lack of information they receive when they start volunteering. I hope you understand that this is not because of a lack of professionalism but due to cultural differences. Also bear in mind that people from high context cultures may find this focus (and perhaps your indignation at the lack of written information) a little insulting, as it may be interpreted as you not having much faith in the integrity of the partner (for us a big jump, for high-context cultures a natural conclusion).

So if you're new in a project, don't get upset that 'nothing is written down'. Take that as a given, and start asking questions (and you may get lucky if there has been a fellow low-context communicator before you who has left instructions!). Don't be afraid to ask for clarification. The fact that your coworkers communicate in a high context doesn't mean that they aren't willing to explain everything to you if you ask! Also, projects that are used to receiving volunteers have usually learned that many foreigners need a more clear and direct way of communication otherwise they don't understand them. However much your coworkers may or may not be used to volunteers who communicate more directly, you should try to tune in to the communication of your coworkers and not assume that everything is ok unless something is vocalized. With a little goodwill on both sides you'll figure everything out in no time!

## 3.2 Language

We have already explained how important it is to speak (some) Spanish or Portuguese when starting your volunteer project. After all, you've chosen to volunteer because you want to have a special experience, and the people you meet will provide that experience for you!

### 3.2.1 At home or in-country?

The first decision you need to make is whether you will learn/ or improve the language before you leave or if you prefer to study once you've arrived in-country. This decision will depend largely on how much time you have before leaving, and how much time you have in your new country. Our personal recommendation is to work on your language skills in the country where you'll be volunteering. This is why; firstly, it gives you a 'soft' entrance into your new life. Volunteering is hard work, both physically and mentally, and you'll have enough changes you'll have to get used to. Starting off your stay in a new country by taking a language course is a very good way to 'ease' into the experience. Why is that? Because at a language school you'll meet other foreigners so you can explore your new country together and take a break from the Spanish sometimes.

The language school staff also organizes lodging for you, so you know you're taken care of from the start. Every language school pays a lot of attention to cultural differences so you'll have fewer surprises when starting your volunteer work. Lastly, if you learn the language in the country where you'll be using it, you'll learn the accent and colloquialisms of that country. Latin America is a huge continent and the Spanish spoken is by no means the same in all countries! Now don't be afraid that Spanish speakers from other countries don't understand you (see side bar) – that isn't the case. You just learn to understand your new colleagues much better.

> Note on language differences between the various Spanish speaking countries; don't be afraid that you'll learn a type of Spanish that nobody outside of your new country understands!
>
> First of all, in the beginning, you'll have the accent of your home country and nothing more. Later, you will use the style of speaking, accent and slang of your host country. This does not mean that other Spanish-speakers won't understand you. At most, they will ask you where you've learned your Spanish. I learned my Spanish in Guatemala and when I went to Mexico after 6 months, I just had a Dutch accent. After living in Guatemala for 2 years I traveled to Costa Rica, where people asked me if I'd learned my Spanish in Guatemala. They understood me perfectly but I used some words that they knew are typically Guatemalan. Then, I moved to Madrid where I didn't understand the Madrileños but again, they understood me perfectly. Here, I made a second jump in language learning and after 2 years living in Madrid, I spoke like a Madrileña and had lost my typical Dutch accent. Everybody knew I wasn't Spanish as I still had a bit of an accent, but nobody could pinpoint it. They only thing they knew for sure was that I lived in Madrid! I took that as a huge compliment – and this was only achieved after 4 years of daily practicing and very hard work.

On the other hand, if you have only limited time abroad due to other commitments, it's a good idea – and of course it's fun! – to prepare for your volunteering by taking a language course where you live. If you're still a student, you can often take a language course at your university, sometimes even for free. Otherwise you could look into courses taught at community colleges, community centers or other such institutions. Then you have the commercial language schools, and (semi-)private tutors. I recommend to study with a teacher and other students as this makes learning much more fun, but of course you could also look into internet courses, online tutors or self-study courses. Make sure you pick a course that you know you will complete; otherwise it's a waste of your time and money, besides the obvious detail that you really need to learn the language before you start your volunteering to get most out of the experience!!!

In financial terms, the cost of taking a course in your home country or taking one in the host country are very comparable. In terms of money spent for skills gained, a total immersion course in a Spanish speaking country is the most cost-effective way to master a language.

### 3.2.2 Some tips on language learning:

1. Start learning basic words: If you are an absolute beginner, at least learn some basics like: "Please", "Thank you", "Where is... ", "How much... ", etc.

Knowing these words breaks the ice at a first meeting.

For intermediate or advanced speakers, we

recommend learning as much vocabulary as possible before you go. The more vocabulary you know, the more you can say. Even if you're not applying the correct grammar, at least you can get your point across.

2. Be able to conjugate important verbs: to have (tener), to do (hacer), to want (querer), to be (ser), to go (ir). Using these verbs combined with a verb allows you to say almost anything you want. For example, instead of 'I saw that play' you can say 'I went to see the play'. In Spanish: 'Ví esta obra de teatro', compared to 'Fui a ver esta obra de teatro'. If you are an absolute beginner focus on the "I" and "you" forms of these verbs.

3. Think the language: Don't try and translate everything word for word. It doesn't work! You will drive your self crazy looking for a word that may not exist in the target language. Try to think in the target language with the words you know. It will be much easier to communicate and you won't get half as frustrated. So what if you find yourself thinking 'Hmmm yo quiero mojado carne con lechuga y papas horno' (Hmmm I want wet steak with lettuce and potato–oven') instead of 'Hmmm I fancy a juicy, medium-rare T-bone steak with a side of mixed salad and potato-gratin'.

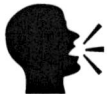

4. When in doubt, "Literature-ize": think of difficult words and use these. For example 'need' doesn't

translate directly into Spanish, but necessity turns into "necesidad", requisite becomes "requisito" and exigency "exigencia." Since these words sound very similar, you will be understood. Romance languages are similar: If you know another romance language, you can use your knowledge of that language for learning Spanish or Portuguese, as many words sound very similar.

5. See the humorous side of it. Don't be afraid to make mistakes, they are great to learn from and can be funny too! As long as you're speaking, you're doing well. Those who learn the fastest are the people who are not afraid to practice their skills. So what if you say something funny? It's the best way to make friends!

### 3.2.3 Just in case

The *Spanish* speaking countries in Latin America are:
Argentina; Bolivia; Chile; Colombia; Costa Rica; Cuba; Dominican Republic; Ecuador, El Salvador; Guatemala; Honduras; Mexico; Nicaragua; Panama; Paraguay; Peru; Puerto Rico; Uruguay and Venezuela.

*Portuguese* is spoken in: Brazil

*English* is spoken in: Belize and many Caribbean countries –these are outside of the scope of this book.

## 3.3 Finances

This paragraph deals with the practicalities of money and finances in Latin America.

### 3.3.1 Currency

I wonder if there will be any reader who hadn't realized this, but for the sake of being absolutely thorough; almost every Latin American country has its own currency. Exceptions are Ecuador, El Salvador and Panama, where the US Dollar is legal tender (officially accepted currency). In Belize, the Belize Dollar is pegged (tied, connected) to the US Dollar at a fixed rate of 2:1. However, even if there is no official recognition of the US Dollar as legal tender, you can use US Dollars in most Latin American countries for certain transactions.

Because many Latin American economies are unstable, their currency tends to fluctuate strongly against other currencies, and can see very steep inflation. Therefore, valuable items (such as cars, real estate, and businesses) are commonly valued in US Dollars and often transactions also take place in that currency. Sometimes the use of the more stable and less inflation-sensitive US Dollar is extended to any purchase over US$50 or so. If this is the case, you as a volunteer will also come into contact with US dollar pricing and payments. You will see prices for excursions, your lodging, flights and sometimes hotel nights quoted in US Dollars. When you see a price quoted in Dollars, you can usually pay in US Dollars as well (and more and more you can use Euros as well). When bringing US Dollars, make sure you take new-looking bills in smaller denominations (most business will not be able to/ want to give you change for a $100 bill) without markings or tears.

Everyday purchases you will make in the local currency. Think about travel expenses, meals, drinks, clothing and souvenirs. To be able to integrate quickly and not pay over the odds for everyday items before leaving or during your first days in the country, make a small list of common price levels (let's say 5, 10, 25, 50, and 100) to what those amounts are worth in your own currency. Then, learn this list by heart. It will make you that much more comfortable when boarding a bus, negotiating a taxi or ordering a coffee. You need to know quickly what things cost and what is reasonable.

## 3.3.2 How to get to your money

For obvious risk and security reasons, we recommend that you do NOT take all the money you will need during your travels in cash with you. Take enough to get through the first week or so, and then rely on other sources to take out cash as you need it. In Latin America, things are less reliable than back home. Therefore, don't count on just 1 source of cash. Traveler's checks have long been a great way of accessing money while traveling. You could sometimes pay for your purchases with them (especially in the tourism industry), they were widely transferable to cash, and they are insured against loss and theft. Nowadays, travelers' checks are less used as other methods of obtaining cash are becoming more common.

Personally, I happily rely on ATM machines. Every decent-sized town in Latin America has ATM machines. The only thing is that you wouldn't use the ATM in Latin America the same way you would back home. First, they are unreliable, frequently out of order or simply empty. Therefore you always need to (try to) get cash long before you run out. You should also try to use the ATM during the day – don't forget you are a target for pick pocketing just because you are foreign so you shouldn't make it any easier for thieves by taking out money at night/ in quiet corners/ in a very busy street where you wouldn't notice somebody brushing up to you.

 To be able to use ATMs in foreign countries, your debit card should be enabled for use abroad. Many banks do this automatically but it couldn't hurt to check up on this. While you are doing that, also check on the fees for taking out money from a foreign cash machine. These can be so steep that you will want to limit your use as much as possible!

Be aware of the difference between drawing cash on your debit card and taking a cash advance on your credit card. Call or visit your bank and get informed of all charges and costs involved. Many credit cards allow you to take out money from a cash machine but charge such ridiculously high amounts for this service (and interest on the money until the next settlement) that you'll only want to do that in case of emergencies.

The advantage of the credit card is that you can pay with it in more and more places in Latin America. VISA is still much more widely accepted (in Latin America) than MasterCard, so if you are thinking of taking out a new card, you might want to bear that in mind. You cannot use it everywhere such as in the USA, but you can certainly pay for excursions, flights, most hotels and for other large expenses with your card.

### 3.3.3 Paying and Negotiating

You probably already know that negotiating prices is very common in Latin American countries. This doesn't mean that you

 can negotiate everything, everywhere. Customs also vary per country, but generally, if there is a cash register you can't negotiate much. For example; public transportation generally has fixed prices but you need to negotiate taxi fares. And in a supermarket you pay the published price but in the market you negotiate.

Some people are better in negotiating and get more fun out of it than others, but even if you don't like it, do try to negotiate in the obvious places. Not even so much because of the actual costs (often it is a few Dollars/ Euros) but more because it is expected and part of the culture. If you really don't feel comfortable, try to respond to the named price with at least 1 counter offer, which will always immediately be met with a new (lower) price, which you can then decide whether to pay or not.

An other part of the culture is a greater tolerance for accepting money without giving/doing anything in return. I am aware that I am making broad generalizations so it is very likely that your individual experience is different (as I explained in chapter 3.1, the differences between individuals are much greater than the differences between cultures). Just the same you need to be aware of this possibility. Especially if you pay for services in advance it can happen (more than in Anglo-Saxon countries) that you will never receive the services. So if you pay for lodging in advance, ask for a receipt where it clearly states that you've paid and for which dates. And if you use a taxi, pay when you arrive. If you order artisan objects, you may pay a small amount in advance (a 'señal') to show you're serious, but the bulk of the sum should be paid upon receiving the finished piece.

## 3.3.4 Tourist vs. Local prices

If you feel a little uncomfortable negotiating knowing that a few dollars (or cents) don't make much difference to you but a huge difference to the seller, it can help to remember that you are paying 'tourist' prices anyway. Those areas that see a lot of tourists usually have a three-tier pricing system. Locals pay certain prices for taxi's, food in the market and daily necessities (depending a little on how hard they haggle). Then, tourists pay 50-100% more for the same goods (again, after negotiating). You, as a volunteer, fall into the third category – at least, you could if you're lucky, sensitive to the culture and speak decent Spanish! Yes, there is a price level for 'foreigners living here', which is roughly 20% more than the local prices. Fair enough, we generally do have a bit more to spend anyway. To be considered a foreigner-who-lives-here, you need to speak Spanish, show cultural sensitivity (meaning you behave 'normal' in the locals' eyes) and you need to be known. So if you go to the market, find your favorite stalls, frequent them and make small talk with the vendor. Be nice and friendly and consistent and you will notice over the course of several weeks or months that the prices you pay drop significantly!

## 3.3.5 Earning money in Latin America

Over the years I have spoken to many prospective volunteers who were very anxious to leave as soon as possible for their volunteer adventure, and were planning on making some extra money in-country. Without exception, I do not recommend this! First of all, it's illegal to work in a country where you don't have a work permit. For some people this is not a very convincing argument, so on to reason #2; it is very difficult to find a paid job. Most Latin

American countries suffer from high unemployment rates and would very much prefer to give available jobs to people they know than to transient foreigners. The only type of job you could get is the type for which they cannot find locals – and this generally involves speaking English. If your English is not fluent it will be even more difficult to find something. So, you could find a position teaching English or you may find work in a restaurant or bar where a lot of foreigners come. Of course you will be expected to commit for a certain period of time to ensure continuity. Then, reason #3 for not counting on funding your stay by working: If you're hired in-country you can only expect to be paid a local salary, which is usually $5-$10 per day for a full-time position.

For most of us, leaving 1 month later than planned and using that month to work as much as possible (think 2 jobs) would – even if you'd work at your local minimum wage – render easily 10 times as much as if you'd be lucky enough to find a fulltime job in Latin America. Besides, would you really want to work full time? You'd probably be more interested to work only a few weeks and/or part time. It's just not worth it! Enjoy the fact that you are lucky enough to live in a country where minimum wage is at a level where most university-educated Latin Americans can only dream of!

## 3.4 Logistics

### 3.4.1 Do you need a visa?

The most important factors to determine if you need a visa are: -your own nationality; the length of your stay; and whether you receive any compensation (in money or services) for your work.

Nationality: Check with the consulate of the country of your choice if people from your nationality require a visa to enter the country as a tourist.

Length of stay: If you need to apply for a visa, you will have to state how long you will be in the country, and hopefully you will be granted a visa for your entire stay. If you don't you might have to adjust your plans. If you will be receiving automatic entrance as a tourist, you will be granted a 30, 60 or 90-day (or whatever is customary) stay. Check with the consulate what is the normal amount and adapt your plans if necessary. Some countries condone (they normally don't quite encourage this, so don't be too vocal about this plan when entering the country for the first time) you leaving the country for a couple of days when your time is up and grant you a new 30 (60 or 90)-day stay when returning.

Compensation: Generally you can assume that you will be needing a work visa, or sometimes a special volunteer/internship/work experience visa if you will be receiving compensation in any kind – money or lodging for example, for your work.

As rules and regulations change frequently, we cannot give you firm advice in this book. Please refer to the embassy (website) of the country you want to visit. You can find (email-) addresses here: http://www.worldembassyinformation.com/

Agencies and Intermediaries also tend to have up-to-date information.

Take this step before you do anything else. The costs, level of complication and length of a possible visa application process could very well influence your decision on where to go and how long to stay.

## 3.4.2 Passport

Next bureaucratic step: after researching applicable visa regulations, check the rules and regulations for documents for travel to and from the country of your choice. Some things to take into consideration: Most countries require your passport to be valid for another 6 months after you leave. Some countries, like the USA, have additional requirements (such as your passport being a Machine Readable Passport, and submitting Advance Passenger Information). Other countries can require that you are immunized against certain illnesses.

Find out the requirements, then get your passport out of your drawer and check if you need to renew it. If you don't have a passport yet, apply for one right now and bear in mind it can be several weeks before it will be ready. The same goes for your immunizations – you may need to get these at least 6 weeks before leaving.

> Yes, going abroad for a long time takes lots of preparation!

## 3.4.3 Flight

We recommend that you don't purchase your flight until you know where you can volunteer. Once you've booked your flight you're pretty much set. What if you find out the project of your first choice cannot receive you and you need to consider different dates or your second-favorite project is in a different location altogether?

The best place to find flights these days is on the internet, except when you're planning a gap year or round-the-world trip. For these special tickets it's best to go to a specialized (youth) travel agency.

Every country has its best booking engines, and everybody probably knows expedia.com and orbitz.com. I recommend that you also check this site: www.itasoftware.com. This site doesn't sell tickets (!) - you can only find information. It's not the most customer friendly website in the world but it does show ALL flights – and corresponding prices- from the major airlines. I like this because they don't highlight or suppress certain airlines or install cookies on your computer that increase the prices of flights that you are frequently searching for (yes, this actually happens! See my blog post on the subject). If you find the flight you want to book, you can go to your favorite booking engine and see if they have the same flight at the same price. Alternatively, through clicking on 'more information' on the flight of your choice, write down the booking codes and call a local travel agent that you want them to book that exact flight for you. Before committing, ask the travel agent about any surcharges that they add to the published price you requested.

When to arrive? Most people immediately think; the day before my volunteer work / language classes start. Well, consider arriving a few days early. First of all, often you'll find the cheapest flights if you travel on a Tuesday or Wednesday. With the difference in price alone you can often stay in a very nice hotel in your new country! Then, there is jetlag, altitude sickness and the general adjustment to a new place – which is all very draining. You probably won't have too much energy to fully focus on your work or school. Of course, if you have to, you will! But it's worthwhile to consider if you won't be happier to give yourself a day or two to acclimatize.

## 3.4.4 Accommodation

Depending on where you will be volunteering and if you use the services of an agency or in-country intermediary you can choose from more or less accommodation options or you will have to find something for yourself.

Below we will discuss the most common accommodation options. In general, we recommend that you commit to the shortest possible time, and extend your stay as you go along. This way, if for whatever reason you don't feel comfortable with your initial choice, you can make changes.

### 3.4.4.1 Host families

This is a common option in Latin America. You will receive a private or shared room (generally with an other volunteer, not with a member of the family) in the house of a family and you will take meals with them. Sometimes you'll have a private bathroom but this is not very common in Latin America. The concept behind this type of accommodation is that you will be fully immersed in the local culture and that you'll have ample opportunities to practice your language skills. Contrary to what many people think you won't be treated as a child but more as a guest of the family. You will receive a key to the house so you can come and go as you please, and you will be expected to show the common courtesies a guest would do as well, such as advising your host mother in advance if you won't be present for a meal.

Your host family can help you with practical questions and intercultural issues, and if there is a good connection between you and them it will very soon feel like home away from home!

## 3.4.4.2 Residences

A residence is a dorm-like accommodation where you can stay in a shared or private room with ensuite or shared bathroom facilities, and receive meals. Residences can be as small as 6-10 people or be fully comparable with university dorms where hundreds of people share ample facilities. This type of accommodation is not very common. If you'd want to stay in a residence, ask your agency or in-country intermediary where this is available and how large this is.

Also, you may be tempted to speak English (or any other language you have in common) more than Spanish or Portuguese. This is also true for a residence-setting. If improving your language skills is an important goal for you and you think you may be tempted into speaking English, you should consider a different accommodation type.

## 3.4.4.3 Shared apartments

Often the cheapest accommodation option, here you share a typical apartment with other volunteers. You will share the bathroom(s) and kitchen with your flat mates and will have to arrange your own meals. This option gives you more independence but also means more work (you'll have to do grocery shopping, cooking and keep the apartment clean). Before committing to this, think carefully how suited you are for the 'communal' life – you and your flat mates will have to find a way to live together and keep the apartment in order.

Maybe your flat mates have a party in the apartment the night before you need to get up at 4am to leave for a weekend trip! You'll have to be prepared and willing to deal with these issues.

Again, you may be tempted to speak English (or any other language you have in common) more than Spanish or Portuguese. This is also true for a residence-setting. If improving your language skills is an important goal for you and you think you may be tempted into speaking English, you should consider a different accommodation type.

### 3.4.4.4 Hotel or private apartments

In most town and villages there is at least 1 hotel where you could stay. Especially for long term stays, this option generally works out pretty expensive, but it can be a very comfortable solution. In smaller hotels you may form a good connection with the owner and/or employees and have ample opportunities to practice your language skills and sample the local cooking!

Private apartments can be a good option for the most independent traveler and for long stays where you really want a place of your own.

### 3.4.5 Insurance

Find out options and costs for travel and medical insurance. Start with your current medical insurance. Does it cover medical costs made outside of your country of residence? If so, is there a limitation for how long you can be out of the country and still claim the costs? Will you get the real costs reimbursed or are there limits (assuming you'll be treated in a private hospital in Latin America)? Are medications included?

Once you know this, you can decide if you need additional medical insurance for your trip. Inquire if you can be repatriated back to your own country in case of serious injuries or death. Also check if a family member can come over and stay with you in case of serious injury.

Travel insurance and medical insurance often overlap on certain aspects. Try to avoid being double insured! Depending on what you're planning on bringing and which activities you want to do, you might need additional coverage for your electronic devices (i.e. your laptop and camcorder), dangerous sports and/or volunteer work.

We can't give specific recommendations for insurers, as every country has its own providers. If you use an agency they will be able to make recommendations and they often even have special offers.

## 3.5 Health

### 3.5.1 Vaccinations

Some countries require you to have certain vaccinations, for other countries it's recommended but not mandatory. Whether or not you follow the recommendation depends on your own preferences, the place you'll be volunteering and the length of your stay. If you will be working in the jungle, in close contact with the local population, and/or in a very underdeveloped area it's wise to invest in good protection and we recommend you get all the shots available. If, on the other hand, you'll be working in an office building in Buenos Aires, your risk to get yellow fever or hepatitis B will not be much higher than if you were at home.

As mentioned above- don't wait too long with investigating and deciding if you need/ want vaccinations, as often you need to get them at least 6 weeks before traveling.

Information on recommended and mandatory vaccinations can be found here:
USA: http://www.cdc.gov/vaccines/
UK: http://www.nhs.uk/chq/pages/Category.aspx?CategoryID=67
Australia: http://www.travelclinic.com.au/
Germany: http://tropeninstitut.de/impfung/index.php
The Netherlands: http://www.lcr.nl/

## 3.5.2 Malaria, Dengue fever and other diseases

Especially when traveling to (sub) tropical areas, you may be exposed to serious diseases that do not occur in your home country. Most of these are transmitted by mosquitoes or flies. Malaria and dengue fever are the best known tropical disease but unfortunately there are many others! If you will be staying any length of time in malaria prone areas, your doctor will probably recommend that you take anti-malaria medications. You can inquire about recommended medications at the same place where you will be getting your immunizations.

The best prevention is not getting bitten! If you are going to live in an area where tropical, mosquito or fly-transmitted diseases are prevalent, take precautions. Wear long-sleeved shirts and pants from dusk till dawn, wear socks and closed shoes and use plenty of insect repellent. Make sure that the insect repellent has a high percentage of DEET, as most mosquitoes are not at all impressed by natural repellents. You should also consider sleeping under a mosquito net if you're in a room that is not well-sealed.

Apart from mosquito- and fly transmitted diseases, you can also contract diseases such as Typhoid, Hepatitis A and B, Diphteria or Tuberculosis if you will be in close contact with the local population in areas where these diseases are present. If this will be the case, we recommend that you get vaccinated.

### 3.5.3 (Prescription) Medications

If you use prescription medications here is a warning - these can become an issue!

First of all, some prescription medications contain 'controlled substances' and can be confiscated at customs as there is no free traffic of these substances allowed in many countries. If you have your medication in their original packaging, and a letter from your doctor stating which medications you need, for which condition, which dosis, and that the medication is for personal use only - you usually will be allowed to bring them into the country. There are exceptions so if you're in doubt, check with the embassy.

Secondly, in many countries the amounts of a medication that a doctor can prescribe at one time is limited. How do you make sure you have enough medication to last for the entire time you will be abroad? Discuss this well in advance with your physician and with your medical insurance.

Ask your doctor to write down the generic name or chemical composition of your medication, and take these with you on your trip. If for whatever reason you loose your medication, or if you run out, you can easily obtain a new prescription from a local doctor. Brand names can vary from country to country and the local physician might not know which medication to give you. Needless to say it is best to carry your medications in your carry on luggage when flying. It's too much of a hassle if they would get lost!

## 3.5.4 Food & Drink

After reading the above paragraphs you may have become completely paranoid about your health! This is not necessary, but it is true that us poor Westerners seem to have much less resistance to certain things, mosquito bites for example – I have never seen locals have as many mosquito bites as some foreigners, and yet they walk around in t-shirts and shorts at night. Another thing is food. We get diarrhea from food items that locals can eat without problems. The locals who are in frequent contact with foreigners know this very well and may chuckle about those Westerners with their delicate constitution. Let them have their joke – it is pretty funny actually that we get sick all the time from perfectly healthy food (in their opinion, as they have since long built up resistance to the bacteria that may be present).

Depending on your courage and how long you'll stay in the country, there are two approaches you can take. First is to be very careful of what you eat and drink, and the second approach is to be a lot less careful (without being silly – as some diseases you can catch are very serious) and deal with the consequences until your body builds up resistance.

If you're staying with a host family or in a residence your life is easy. Experienced host families are very familiar with the food preparation requirements for foreigners and you can safely eat and drink anything they prepare for you. You will just need to watch yourself when traveling.

If you live in a shared apartment you need to take sufficient precautions when preparing food. The first thing you need to buy are food disinfectant drops. Any fresh fruits and vegetables that you buy should be 'bathed' in a solution of water and disinfectant drops before you prepare it. It's safe and doesn't leave any taste so you can use it for any food, including lettuce. When preparing food, make sure you follow the hygiene rules to the letter, including frequent hand washing, avoiding cross-contamination and thorough heating of all food.

You shouldn't expect to be able to drink the tap water anywhere in Latin America, but in most areas it's ok to brush your teeth with. Use bottled water as much as possible but it's not necessary to get too worried about getting sick from getting water on your lips when showering.

Now, when you're traveling and eating and drinking from restaurants and stalls that are not used to catering to tourists, you should be very careful. Especially because you are traveling you don't want to get sick. Diarrhea and long-distance bus rides don't mix….

So, the basic rules are: eat nothing that is not thoroughly cooked and served piping hot, and don't drink anything that doesn't come out of a closed, sealed container. When ordering a drink, check if the bottle is sealed and don't be afraid to asked for a closed bottle ('¿Me podría traer una botella cerrada por favor?). It won't be the first time if bottles of water are re-filled with tap water. You just can't run the risk. Oh, and ice cubes are made of water so when in any doubt – avoid them too!

## 3.5.5 If you get ill

Let's hope that it won't happen to you, but if you will get ill you have to know what to do. And you have to bear in mind that if you'll be living in a new country with a completely different climate, food and life style – and that can have an effect on your health.

I hope that you'll follow the recommendations from paragraph 3.4.5 and will select a good medical insurance that will cover (most of) your possible costs. Having a medical insurance does not mean that you can visit the doctor without taking your wallet with you! When you're abroad, you usually need to pre-pay everything, save the receipts, and claim the money from the insurance later.

It's really important that the receipts you're getting state your full name, your complaint, the diagnosis and treatment that the doctor prescribed, and the doctor's full name and license number. Doctors who regularly treat foreigners will know this and automatically give you a form or statement, but if you don't get it you need to ask for it. Your insurance will happily refuse to reimburse you if you submit (in their opinion) incomplete paperwork.

For large medical expenses, such as treatment in a hospital, you may not have to pay cash on-site. For this level of expenses, you need to bring your insurance card (details) and the hospital administration will contact your insurer to arrange payment with them directly. Just the same, you're usually required to give your credit card number as a guarantee. Again, larger, private hospitals in touristy areas are very familiar with these procedures but hospitals in rural areas may not have any experience in dealing with (foreign) insurance companies. All medical insurers (correct me if I'm wrong) will reimburse treatment in private hospitals in developing countries, so try to reach such a hospital if you need help. These hospitals provide a significantly higher standard of care and observe stricter hygiene standards.

Buying medication is a lot easier in Latin America than in most Western countries. It's incredible what pharmacists will sell you over the counter (meaning without a prescription from a physician). Many locals don't visit a doctor very often – they turn directly to the pharmacist for advice. It's up to you to decide how much you trust the pharmacists' opinion but as your medical insurance will reimburse your doctor's bill, we recommend that you take the safe route. At the same time, it's convenient to be able to go to the pharmacy directly if you already know for sure what you need. This can be antibiotics for a urinary tract infection or a refill of your medication for a chronic condition (such as allergy medication). Whenever you buy medication, make sure you understand what you are buying, how to use it and check if the medication has not expired.

An interesting phenomenon that I have discovered in Latin America is that you'll never leave the doctor's office without a prescription. In Guatemala specifically, you even get 3 prescriptions, every single time! Apparently it's a cultural trait that a good doctor gives you medications and that the medication will make you better. However, when you start reading what it exactly is that you've been prescribed, you'll discover that you often get a prescription for a over the counter pain medication and sometimes an other medication that isn't harmful, but also not necessarily helpful. I, for example, once got a prescription for an anti-parasite drug (which I needed), an anti-inflammatory (which I didn't need – I checked with my sister who is a physician) and paracetamol (known as acetaminophen in the USA) (which I had anyway). Conclusion; don't be afraid to ask carefully what the doctor is prescribing and what it is used for.

## 3.6 Safety

Many Latin American countries have a reputation for being dangerous. This reputation is based on real occurrences of course, but it's important to know how to interpret safety warnings. Countries such as Mexico, Guatemala and Brazil have high violent crime and murder rates and this can sound very daunting. Here you need to know that most of these crimes are gang-related and most victims have gang connections. Further, these incidents mostly take place in areas where tourists don't go and touristy areas are usually very well patrolled by police.

Most countries are acutely aware of the value of tourist spending in their country, and will try to make sure that nothing bad happens to them. Therefore, those areas that tourist visit are usually very well guarded and controlled, and sometimes there are even special tourist police who control touristy areas, often speak English and are especially helpful. Also, and you won't find any official information backing this up, in many countries the crime solving rate is very low, due to lack of funding for police forces and investigation, and unfortunately also due to corruption. If a foreigner is harmed, then the pressure to solve the crime is much higher because of the possible consequences for the reputation of the country as a tourist destination. So many criminals wouldn't be too interested in getting entangled with a foreigner.

### 3.6.1 Petty theft

I hope that the above paragraphs have put your mind at ease. Now don't get too comfortable, because although you're often less of a target for serious crimes, you're first in line for petty theft, and pick pocketing! Some of us look very obviously foreign; others could pass for Latin American in features. Even if the latter is the case with you don't be fooled – you'll still immediately be identified as a foreigner! It's the way we dress, look, walk, carry ourselves... we just stand out! By the way, this is truer in rural communities than in large cosmopolitan cities. Anyway, the fact that you're a foreigner makes you an automatic target for theft. As we explained in chapter 1.6, you will be considered by many locals as limitlessly rich, and therefore a prime target for pick pocketing. Accept this reality and take precautions so you lower the risk of being pick pocketed or stolen, and if it happens that it doesn't have great consequences.

**Precautions when traveling:**
- Carry all your valuables in a money belt which you should hide under your clothes.
- If you do need to access your money belt, do this in a bathroom or other private space where nobody can observe you.
- Carry a wallet with just some cash for the day, and use only this wallet to pay for your purchases
- Keep a sharp eye on your belongings, don't leave them out of your sight
- Don't nap when using public transportation, or take turns with a traveling companion
- Don't accept food or drink from strangers on public transportation. They can be laced with a sedative and you may wake up hours later, minus your belongings
- Hide expensive cameras, cell phones and laptops
- In areas where buses or taxis are sometimes held up, don't travel at night
- Follow the advice from experienced travelers, guide books and locals

**Precautions for everyday life:**
- Don't carry your passport, carry only a copy
- Don't carry your credit cards or bank card if you don't think you'll be needing them
- Hide expensive cameras, cell phones and laptops and don't take them with you if you won't be needing them
- Don't get drunk! If your judgment is impaired you might make silly decisions. In Latin America silly decisions can often have very bad consequences, more so than at home.
- Don't accept drinks and food from strangers (see above)
- Don't walk alone at night
- Be aware of scams with fake policemen, dirt on your clothes or a similar distraction. If something weird happens, your immediate reaction should be to put your hand on your purse/wallet and keep it there.

## 3.6.2 Getting robbed

If you happen to be so unlucky to be held up, don't offer any resistance and give up your valuables. You have insurance, you've made copies of all your documents and money is just money. If this happens to you, it will take a little time to get through the necessary paperwork but you will be able to get on with your (volunteer) life. If you resist, fight back or try to flee, you can be met with violence. The resulting physical and mental injuries are far more serious than any lost passport or credit card. Unfortunately, many Latin Americans grow up in environments were violence is much more common than in our countries. This, combined with a desperate personal situation with no possibility for improvement, can lead people to use more violence much quicker than what we are used to. Don't try to be brave.

## 3.6.3 Women travelers

Sometimes women feel more unsafe than men when traveling, especially in macho cultures. It's true, especially in macho cultures males feel this necessity of acknowledging your presence and giving you 'compliments'. These can be very creative and flattering, but unfortunately most males don't go much beyond the catcall or whistle – and that gets old really fast. I find these catcalls easy to ignore on some days, extremely irritating on others, and amusing on occasions, but never threatening. For some reason this is just what males do when they're standing around in the street. We have never heard of a situation where a whistle or comment was meant to threaten a woman or as a preliminary to an assault. The only thing you can do is ignore the guys completely. That's what the local ladies do. If you get mad, or give a reply, they have succeeded in getting your attention and will be even more unrelenting in the future!

At the same time, because we are women and physically less strong than men, we sometimes feel less safe. Then we have the added risk for molestation or rape which can add significantly to unsafe feelings. The best advice I can give is that women follow the safety precautions mentioned in the first paragraph strictly. Contrary to the catcalls in the street, men that you meet in bars can have more improper intentions. Foreign women have the reputation that we engage in sex quite freely. It's not so very surprising as a lot of women tend to more easily engage in a little flirtation or affair when on vacation than back home. I'm not trying to imply that you will do that as well, I just want to point out that the guys do have a bit of a reason for at least wanting to try. Also, especially in more conservative and/or rural areas it's harder to meet local women in bars because most of them are not allowed to go to bars. So, when meeting men in social situations, I recommend that you are very clear and firm if you're not interested, or if someone touches you in a way that you're not comfortable with (especially when dancing Latin American dances guys often take the opportunity to 'explore' a little and see how it is received). This is not the place and time to display indirect communication and extreme politeness so common in the Latin American cultures! In the years and years of living and traveling in Latin American countries and maintaining a very active social life (if you see what I mean) I have never had a bad experience. I did have a policy of never accepting drinks from guys (unless they were friends), never flirting (well, at least not in public ☺ ), never getting drunk and certainly never accepting offers of being escorted home by guys I didn't know very, very well. Especially when I lived in Antigua (where I was for 2 years) people get to know each other, so after a couple of months it was known 'in the scene' that I wasn't available, and I noticed that most men stopped trying so much (they're still Latino's so they will always act friendly and flirty, but I was relieved to get less of the horniness and more of the gentlemanliness of the Latino males!). If you're going to stay in one place for a longer period of time, and you're planning on going out a lot (and why shouldn't you, right?) I can recommend that you invest in a bit of aloofness at first and work from there.

## 3.6.4 Specific challenges for volunteers

Now, volunteers tend to live and work in more residential areas so you need to be extra careful. Lodging for volunteers will never be in the most dangerous areas; organizations and agencies will always make sure that you don't run any necessary risks. Projects, especially social projects, can be located in poorer neighborhoods – logical if you remember that these communities need most help. Again, nobody wants volunteers come to harm so if you work in a rougher area, there will usually be certain safety measures in place. Take them seriously and also follow the advice from coworkers and your host family, in-country contact and agency. These safety measures can be that you shouldn't walk to and from the project in the dark; or that you never walk alone in the area. Many such projects pick up the volunteers from the nearest bus stop at a certain time and they walk as a group to the project. This serves to show the community that you – the volunteer- are there to help the community -this usually guarantees your personal safety.

 You still run the risk to be in the wrong place at the wrong time, especially when you live and work in a non-touristy area where there are safety concerns or social unrest. You should always be aware of your surroundings, not involve yourself in protests or demonstrations, and take the safer option (leave a certain area, take a taxi, not board or leave a bus) when in doubt.

CPSIA information can be obtained at www.ICGtesting.com
Printed in the USA
LVOW10s0004311015

460464LV00030B/779/P